Exploring the Fundamental Features of Translation

Exploring the Fundamental Features of Translation:

A Guide for Specialists and Non-Specialists

By

Nabil Al-Awawdeh

Cambridge Scholars Publishing

Exploring the Fundamental Features of Translation:
A Guide for Specialists and Non-Specialists

By Nabil Al-Awawdeh

This book first published 2023

Cambridge Scholars Publishing

Lady Stephenson Library, Newcastle upon Tyne, NE6 2PA, UK

British Library Cataloguing in Publication Data
A catalogue record for this book is available from the British Library

ISBN (10): 1-5275-1978-3
ISBN (13): 978-1-5275-1978-7

TABLE OF CONTENTS

PREFACE

This book is a detailed guidebook designed for students, teachers, and specialists in translation who want to improve their comprehension of translation problems from an introductory level up to advanced subjects. The book's significance lies in adopting a bottom-up strategy for translation issues. It does not principally confront translation topics as challenges and solutions but rather as significant concerns to translation students and researchers. This approach to translation issues is what gives the manuscript its importance. The guidebook covers essential subjects that are derived from both historical and contemporary considerations regarding translation. Due to this, students and other researchers will be able to implement their comprehension of the subjects that have been addressed in a variety of settings. In addition, this book contains six segments, each of which addresses concerns regarding translation at a different level of the target language.

The first chapter is primarily an introduction segment that delves into various foundational translation-related subjects. This chapter takes a broad look at how translation and activities related to translation have remained an integral part of the communication mechanisms used daily among individuals whose linguistic backgrounds are distinct from one another. Because of its significance, translation has been the subject of a wealth of research investigating the field's practical and theoretical aspects. This helps to differentiate academic investigations from those conducted in other areas of the globe. The purpose of this section of the book is to elaborate on a unified conception of translation, explain the history of translation and the emergence of translation as an academic discipline, and talk about the tenets of translation studies as well as the essence of translation studies in terms of theoretical development.

In the second chapter, we take a look at various times in the history of translation. This discussion examines, from diverse historical distinct perspectives, the contention that translation has been around for at least as long as the human species and the advent of communication. This chapter further explains that translation has been an essential factor in transmitting culture, concepts, philosophy, and perspectives throughout human history. However, the regionalization of the history of translation has dominated discussions of the history of translation, producing ideas such as the history of translation in the Western world and the history of translation in the Asian world, among other regionalized documentations. This has resulted in discussions of the history of translation being dominated by regionalization.

This chapter offers a comprehensive comprehension of how the history of translation as a means of communication has not followed any anticipated path. The chapter includes a discussion of translation activities during specific periods, as well as the characteristics of translation activities during those eras. The history of translation can be broken down into sections corresponding to various periods in human existence. This chapter elaborates on the character of translation activities that took place during the BC era until the period referred to in the scientific community as "Classical Antiquity," which lasted from 1–499. In addition, activities related to translation during the medieval period, the 16th century, and up to the patterns of the 21st century are covered in this chapter. In the previous section, we addressed how activities related to translation in the 21st century have concentrated on the utilization of technological tools to make translation easier.

The development of various theories regarding translation is the primary emphasis of the third chapter. In the first attempt, we made an effort to highlight the distinction that exists between "translation theory" and "theories of translation" by drawing a comparison between the two phrases. The first aspect is a chronological transformation of translation as anthropogenic activity, from a practical act of translating texts to a theoretical activity of studying the fundamentals of translation from a broad range of perspectives; on the other hand, the second aspect encompasses a formulated conceptual model for the practical translation and survey of translation through certain viewpoints. To put it another way, the latter involves the development of a structure for the actual translation process as well as the study of translation from a variety of viewpoints. Translation theory is the field that ignited the interest and aspiration that led to the formulation of theories of translation. The combination of these two factors led to the development of this field. The theories of translation that are examined in this chapter are approached from three different vantage points: from historical or chronological perspectives, from individual schools of thought, and from a locational perspective. The philological theory, the linguistic theory, and the functional component in translation were all addressed from a historical point of view. The theories of translation developed by Dryden and Catford, as well as the theory of translation proposed by Nida, the theory of translation developed by Susan Bassenet and Andre Levefre, and the theory of translation proposed by Venuti, are extensively discussed. These theories came from individual schools of thought. There are several different theories of translation, each of which is predicated on the actions that took place at particular times and places throughout history. The Chinese translation theory, the Asian translation theory, and the Western theory of translation are the three primary regions that are investigated in this book.

The various strategies for translation are the topic of discussion in chapter four. The multiple systems which conceived different approaches to problem-solving issues of thought are the primary emphasis. The work of a particular group of researchers is observed and demonstrated by examining several other studies on translation. This portion of the guidebook presents the translation techniques that were recommended by Vinay and Darbelnet (1973), Venuti (1995), Desline (1993), Malone (1988), and Newmark (1988).

The various ideas that make up the nature of translation are dissected in detail in chapter five. The study of translation, along with its numerous practical implementations, has, over several years, resulted in the development of several foundational principles that support the discipline of translation in its broadest meaning. These principles include the following: the concept of fidelity, as well as fidelity erosion, transparency, equivalence, terminology, and both machine translation and technical translation, are all included in these concepts. The list is not limited to the concepts listed above, but these are the ones that are explored in this chapter.

The final chapter investigates the factors determining whether translation can be classified as applied translation. This chapter demonstrates that translation theory and practice have always been fundamental components of applied linguistics. This is one of the main arguments that the chapter puts forward. The endeavor made by contemporary translators to share essential translation activities between human and computer translators has been investigated by researchers in the field of translation theories. Since the most recent developments in translation are centered on the utilization of technology, this narrative aims to explain how artificial intelligence could assist human translators during the translation process. From the perspective of the primary emphasis placed on technology in translation, this chapter investigates fundamental questions concerning the acknowledgment of translation as an applied discipline.

CHAPTER ONE

INTRODUCTION

1.1. What is Translation

Generally, translation and translation activities have consistently remained part of daily communication mechanisms among speakers of different linguistic backgrounds. The importance of translation has necessitated a plethora of studies exploring both the practical and theoretical dimensions of the domain, distinguishing scholarly explorations from other parts of the world. In this part of the book, our concern is to expound on a unified conception of translation, explicate the history of translation and the emergence of translation as an academic discipline, and discuss the tenets of translation studies and the essence of translation studies in theoretical development.

1.2. The Conception of Translation

Many authors have proposed their interpretations of translation to converge on a single, agreed-upon meaning for the term "translation." The acts of conveying a text in one language context and producing, developing, constructing, or giving an equivalent in another language background have been the primary emphasis in translation up to this point. According to Newmark (1988), translation is generally, but not constantly, seen as conveying the meanings of a message in a different language in the manner the originator desired the text to be understood. However, this definition is not always accurate. This manner of conceptualizing translation gives the impression that the process is straightforward since it suggests that a person should be able to communicate the same thing in both of their languages. Newmark stressed further that this idea might be considered convoluted, unnatural, and deceptive because speakers of a second language purport to be somebody they are not when they speak the first language. It is important to note that Newmark's perspective on translation is limited since it simply addresses the translator's activity. It does not take into account any of the other essential characteristics of the operations, and it makes a simplified extrapolation of the linguistic individuality of the translator. To provide a more comprehensive understanding of translation, Munday (2007) acknowledged that the term "translation" itself might have a variety of interpretations depending on the viewpoint. On the one hand, it might relate to the topic matter in general, the product, or the content which has been translated. On the other hand, it might also allude to the procedure, the action of doing the translation, which is more often referred to as translating.

Relatively, Catford (1978) focused on the procedure for translation and the unending debate on equivalency. Catford asserted that translation remains the substitution of textual content text from one language with textual material written in another language equivalent to the Source Language text. Baker (2004), Nida (1978), and Hatim (2004) invariably followed the conception of translation by Catford, which is a shift away from the possibility of understanding translation from the views of the activity of translating and from the standpoint of what was produced. As such, we argue that translation is better understood as a product and activity.

Simpsons and Wiener (1989) explained that translation is the transformation from one language to another or the representation of one item in another. According to Hornby (2010), the term "translate" refers to either conveying the meaning of a text or spoken word into another language or the product of such a process. Venuti (1995), writing from a closely related traditional point of view, proposed that translation is the operation by which the sequence of signifiers that encompasses the original message is represented by a succession of signifiers in the chosen language, whereby the translator delivers based on an inference.

1.3. Basic Concepts in Translation

Some concepts are traditionally recognized as basic terms that are invariably utilized in a discussion of translation as a product as an activity. Some of these terms are discussed mainly to provide readers with an understanding of the fundamental terms predominantly used in translation.

i.   Source language (SL) and source language text: The source language is generally known as the language in which the main text was written. It is the language that provides the original text. The source language text is considered the author's original thought rendered in a written form.

ii. Target language (TL) and target language text: The target language, which some authors have referred to as the secondary language, is the linguistic background wherein a translator transfers the meanings, thoughts, and conceptions of the original text. The target language may not necessarily be the translator's first language, but it is not the language in which the original text was primarily produced. A reproduction of the source language text in the target language is referred to as the target text. One primary concern in the production of the source text is the issue of equivalence. At the same time, some authors maintain that the translator's focus is to keep the message style and sociolinguistic nuances of the source text, while others insist that the focus of translation is to satisfy the communication need of a particular target audience. As such, what is considered the equivalent of the source text is relative, considering the divergent perspectives.

iii. The translator: Traditionally, the translator renders the source text into the target language. Beyond this conventional perception of a translator, many authors have argued that a translator is also an author since translation involves creating a new text. Although the idea and thought may be generated from the source text, the translator reproduces the source in another language, which some researchers consider a unique text; the translator is viewed as a writer.

Other essential concepts in translation include the translation processes, which have been described using different terms such as "rendering" (Colina, 2015), "transferring" (Munday, 2007), and "creating" (Baker, 2004), among other terms. The differences in the conception of translation processes are mainly associated with the interpretation of equivalency, faithfulness, and fidelity erosion. Strong emphasis on maintaining the meaning and message of the original text remains the center of the debate.

1.4. Fundamental Concerns in Translation Studies

Throughout the history of human civilization, printed and spoken translations have served a vital role in interpersonal language, not the least of which has provided access to significant texts for the sake of academic study and religious practice. However, the recognition of translating as an area of study did not start in earnest until around 60 years ago. Before then, translation had typically been seen as little more than a side activity during language study in contemporary language classes. In actuality, beginning in the late 19th century and continuing into the 1960s, the grammar-translation technique was the predominant approach in secondary schools throughout many nations to teach foreign languages. The fact that translation is often geared toward linguistic education and training may help explain, at least in part, why academic circles acknowledge translation as of subordinate significance. Assessments in translation were often recommended to those who wanted to acquire a new language or read a text written in a foreign language before they had the linguistic capacity to read the work in its original form. Once a student had developed the required abilities to read the text in its original form, it was often frowned upon for them to study a work available only in translation.

This academic field is now more often recognized as translation studies anywhere English is spoken. The writings of James S. Holmes, an esteemed American translation scholar, are often cited as the inspiration for modern translation studies. In the critical paper that defined the field, which Holmes presented in 1972 but did not make broadly accessible until 1988, he identified the then-emerging field as being associated with "the sophistication of challenges huddled beneath the circumstance of the translation process and translating." Holmes's publication was delivered in 1972. In the first edition of Snell-Hornby's book, *Translation Studies: An Integrated Approach*, published in 1988, the author stated that "the proposal that translation studies should be considered as an autonomous field has emerged from numerous sources in recent years" (Snell-Hornby, 1988, p.ii).

Two particularly obvious facets that have contributed to the increased visibility of translation studies are evident in the literature. There has been an explosion in the number of specialized translation and interpretation courses offered at both the undergraduate and postgraduate levels. These programs, which draw in thousands of learners each year, are primarily geared toward the education of prospective competent corporate translators and translators. Additionally, they serve as highly valuable entry-level credentials for translating and translating.

Linguistics, the academic field that focuses on language study in general, has conflicted with the development of Translation Studies as a separate theoretical realm, which has been the subject of much dispute. When we study linguistics, we get access to resources that allow us to develop more nuanced descriptions of the target language for translation. Recently, however, there have been debates within the nascent field of translation studies concerning whether linguistic reports are helpful. There is a common assumption in the recent translation literature that translation studies may be divided into two distinct camps (Baker, 1996; Venuti, 1996). For starters, there's the "linguistically oriented" perspective, which is based on extensive linguistic research. The second, known as the "cultural" perspective, is grounded in historical investigations and critical theory fields. At a specific time, it was generally agreed that translation study was a significant linguistics subfield (Baker, 2000). In recent years, it has been acknowledged more and more as a distinct field of study, while it has been questioned how heavily it should rely on linguistics. Some academics argue that translation studies need to move away from linguistics in favor of more historically and culturally grounded research methods. Is it even feasible to separate linguistics and translation studies?

In the decades of the 1950s, 1960s, and 1970s, linguistics was already widely accepted as a legitimate academic topic of study. However, translation was still fighting for its own identity. As a result of the necessity for a guiding theoretical framework and the fact that language is the primary focus of both translation and linguistics, linguistics has become the primary source of the theoretical foundation for translation studies. Earlier investigations into the translation process tended toward a prescriptive approach and a very superficial exploration of meaning. It's worth noting that back then, there weren't nearly as many methods that sought to describe or provide explanations as there are now. The focus on language allowed for the development of easily digestible guidelines and potential solutions for translators to use when encountering linguistic obstacles. Problems like a lack of equivalence at the word level or culturally specific things were seen as primarily formal in character. Translation studies had been thought of as a subfield of applied linguistics for this reason rather than as a distinct field in its own right, even if one was still in its infancy. This is still the opinion of several linguists and academics. The work of Bell (1991) is one example. Within "a broadly defined applied linguistics", he hopes to develop "an intellectually pleasing and practically effective theory of translation" (Bell, 1991). Ironically, those associated with the language paradigms are the most vocal advocates for recognizing "Translation Studies" as a distinct academic field. Many consider linguistics an important, if not the most important, source of data and information in translation studies.

Works cited

Colina, S. (2015) Fundamentals of Translation. Cambridge University Press.

Baker, M., and Saldanha, G (2000) Routledge Encyclopedia of Translation Studies, London: Routledge.

Baker, M. (1996) In Other Words: A Coursebook on Translation. London and New York: Routledge.

Baker, M. (2004) Translation and Conflict: A Narrative Account. Abingdon: Routledge.

Catford, I. (1977) A Linguistic Theory of Translation. Oxford: Oxford
   University Press.
Bell, R.T. (1991) Translation and Translating, Theory and Practice,
   Longman.
Hatim, B. (2004) Discourse and the Translator. London: Longman.
Munday, J. (2007) Introducing Translation Studies: Theories and
   Applications. Routledge.
Newmark, P. (1988) A Textbook of Translation. New York and London:
   Prentice-Hall.
Nida, E. (1978) Towards a Science of Translating. Leiden: E. J. Brill.
Snell-Hornby, M. (2006) The Turns of Translation Studies, Amsterdam and
   Philadelphia: John Benjamins.
Venuti, L. (1996) The Translation Studies Reader. Oxon: Routledge.
Venuti, L. (1995) The Translator's Invisibility. A History of Translation,
   London and New York: Routledge.

CHAPTER TWO

INSIGHTS INTO THE HISTORY OF TRANSLATION AND THE EMERGENCE OF TRANSLATION STUDIES

Across different historical projections, translation has been argued to be as old as the human race and communication. Translation has been instrumental in transmitting culture, thoughts, ideology, and perceptions across ages. However, the regionalization of the translation history has dominated discussions of the history of translation, producing ideas such as the "history of translation in the Western world" (Nida and Taber, 1969) and the "history of translation in the Asian world", among other regionalized documentations.

Traditionally, the history of translation as a means of communication has not been organized along any projected approach. What is dominant is the discussion of translation activities in specific periods and the nature of translation activities in those periods. This latter approach is adopted here, as the history of translation is subdivided across different periods in human existence.

2.1. Translation Activities in the BC Era

According to most historical records, the beginning of translations may be dated back to 196 BC. The Rosetta Stone is an important historical artifact used during the early stages of language translation. The Rosetta Stone wasn't discovered until 1799, although it was commissioned by the ruler of Egypt at the time, Ptolemy, to be etched by monks at the Memphis Temple as a show of support for the monarch. The inscription on the Rosetta Stone is in three separate languages: ancient Greek, hieroglyphics (which is the name given to the Egyptian language), and Demotic, which is the name given to the local Egyptian character. The modern academic community can grasp hieroglyphs as a result of this interpretation. Saint Jerome, a prominent theologian and historian known as "the patron saint of translators" is credited with making the first Latin translation of the Bible, originally written in Hebrew and Greek, somewhere around the year 300 BC. We now observe the World Day of Translation every year on September 30, the anniversary of the day he passed away. Several authors have begun their explorations into the history of translation by focusing on his period as their point of departure.

It is documented that translation was practised as far back as the Mesopotamian period, when the Sumerian poem Gilgamesh was rendered into Asian languages. This is the first known instance of translation. This was written sometime in the middle of the 2nd millennium BC. When researching the history of translation, some of the first literary works discovered include the Septuagint, which dates back to 2100 BC and contains The Epic of Gilgamesh, as well as St. Jerome's translation of the Bible. It is thought that these two works were the first to be translated. After Buddhist monks transferred sutras into Chinese mandarin, this was a pivotal moment in the historical translation record since Asia translation played an important role. According to the facts that emerged from researching a concise history of translation, the primary function of early translation seems to have been the widespread dissemination of religious views. Clay tablets were employed in approximately 2500 BC to read symbols from the ancient Semitic languages of Sumerian and Eblaite. These languages belonged to the Semitic language family.

Because of the long-standing tradition of translating material among Egyptian, Mesopotamian, Syriac, Anatolian, and Hebrew, the Sumerian *Epic of Gilgamesh* (circa 2000 BCE) is considered to be an older icon for the art of translation. This epic poem from Ancient Mesopotamia is often generally viewed as the oldest known great book of literature translated by predecessors into Southwest Asian languages. It was written in the ancient language of Sumer. The "Treaty of Kadesh" was written in 1274 BCE and is the oldest ancient Near Eastern treatise for which both the Egyptian and Hittite versions have been preserved. It is a bilingual Egyptian-Hittite treatise and is considered to be a third icon for the art of translation.

It is generally agreed that the Greek translation of the Hebrew Bible, which took place in the 3rd century BC was the first significant translation in the Western world. Because the scattered Jewish people had lost their ability to speak Hebrew, the language of their ancestors, they needed a Greek translation of the Bible to be capable of reading it. This translation is known as the "Septuagint", which is a word that relates to the 70 translators who have been entrusted with translating the Hebrew Bible in Alexandria, Egypt. The Hebrew Bible was translated into Greek at the same time. According to the tradition, each translator was kept in isolated seclusion in a separate cell while working on the translation, and all seventy versions turned out to be identical. The "Septuagint" eventually evolved into the role of the source text for subsequent translation into Latin, Coptic, Armenian, and Georgian, amongst other languages. In the two centuries that followed, biblical materials initially written in Hebrew were also brought to Alexandria to be translated into Greek.

The paucity of comprehensive historical sources showing the precise nature of translation efforts throughout the BC era stands out as crucial in the history of translation during that era. The translators themselves, the components that were translated, the kind of language writing system employed throughout the translation process, and any other notable aspects were the primary focus of attention.

2.2. Translation in The Years 1–499

Conventionally, the years 1–499 BC are considered part of the period known as "Classical Antiquity". Classical antiquity, also known as the classical era, classical period, or classical age, is a historical period in ancient history that spans from the 8th century BC to the 5th century AD and is centered around the Mediterranean Sea. It includes the intertwined settlements of prehistoric Greece and old Rome, collectively referred to as the Greco-Roman world. During this time, Greek and Roman societies were at the height of their power and exerted significant influence throughout a substantial portion of Europe, Northern Africa, and Western Asia.

It is widely projected that early translation begins with Homer's epic poetry, which was written in Greece during the 8th and 7th centuries BC, and continues through the development of Christianity in the 1st century AD and the collapse of the Western Roman Empire in the 4th century AD (5th-century AD). It comes to an end with the fall of classical civilization during late antiquity, which spans the years 250–750 and overlaps with the early medieval period (600–1000). This enormous time and geographical range encompass a vast variety of distinct civilizations and time eras. Classical antiquity could alternatively refer to an idealistic view of what was, as described by Edgar Allan Poe, "the splendor that was Greece, and the majesty that was Rome" (Venuti, 2008), held by those who lived far later in history. Numerous historical records on the actions of translation in the years 1–499 were predominantly projected from the viewpoint of religious engagements. These texts include a vast amount of information. During this period, the most important activity was the Bible's translation into other languages. The period beginning before Christ's birth and continuing until the 2nd or 3rd century AD was when literary and religious texts were translated into other languages. Hebrew literature and manuscripts were translated into ancient Greek so that others may read them. By the 5th century, the Old Testament had been translated into ancient Greek, along with other works of literature such as epics, tragedies, comedies, hymns, and prose tales, among other works.

When Buddhist monks first began translating sutras into Chinese languages, translation in Asia played an essential part in the historical period of translation. This was during the era covered by this particular history. According to the facts that emerged from researching a concise history of translation, the primary function of early translation seems to have been the widespread dissemination of religious views. Kumrajva was a Buddhist monk, scholar, and translator who lived in China in the late 4th century. He is most known for his enormous task of translating Buddhist writings originally written in Sanskrit into Chinese, which he accomplished in a prolific manner. His translation of the *Diamond Sutra*, which is revered and studied in Zen Buddhism, is considered to be his most notable work. The *Diamond Sutra* is a Mahayana sutra prominent in East Asia. In accordance with the websites of the British Library, "the oldest completed survival of a printed book" is a later copy of the Chinese translation of *Diamond Sutra* dated 868. The translations of Kumarajva had a significant impact on Chinese Buddhism. These translations were simple and plain, with an emphasis more on communicating the content than on providing an exact literal portrayal. His translations enjoyed more popularity than others that came after them that was more literal.

The dissemination of Buddhism across Asia resulted in massive translation projects carried out continuously for longer than a thousand years, and in other instances, in a concise amount of time. The Tanguts, for example, could translate volumes that had taken the Chinese centuries to solve in a matter of decades. This was possible for two reasons: first, they took advantage of the newly invented block printing method, and second, they enjoyed the full support of the government. Contemporary sources describe the Monarch and his family individually making contributions to the translation initiatives, along with sages of various nationalities.

After the Arabs had captured the Greek Empire, they also made significant efforts to translate all of the scientific and philosophical writings that the Greeks had produced into Arabic. These translations took a very long time.

2.3. Translation in the Medieval Period (500–1499)

The post-classical era roughly corresponds to the period known as the Middle Ages or the medieval period in the history of humanity. The Middle

Ages, or medieval era, spanned essentially through the 6th century to the late 15th. The collapse of the Western Roman Empire marked the beginning of this period, followed by the Renaissance and the Discovery Era. It was formerly thought that the Middle Ages were a time of unbroken obscurity, mysticism, and social injustice; however, modern scholars today recognize that this period was a vibrant time in which the concept of Europe as a unique cultural entity originated. In late antiquity and the early Middle Ages, governmental, socio-cultural, and institutional formations were profoundly reorganized. This occurred as Roman expansionist customs fell away to those of Germanic civilizations who created empires in the lands that had formerly been part of the Western Empire. Even more spectacular expansion occurred throughout the latter part of the Middle Ages, sometimes known as the high Middle Ages. This was a time of population and urban growth, economic and geographical expansion, the establishment of a national character, and the reorganization of secular and religious institutions. All of these developments defined the era. It was the time of the Crusade, Mediaeval architecture and art, ecclesiastical authority, the beginning of the universities, the rediscovery of ancient Greek ideas, and the ascent of intellectual accomplishments to new heights.

Throughout the Medieval Era, Latin served as the de facto international language of scholarship in the Western world since there was so little translation of Latin writings into native languages. Alfred the Great, King of Wessex in England, was well ahead of his time in the 9th century when he commissioned vernacular translations from Latin into English of Bede's *Ecclesiastical History* and Boethius' *The Consolation of Philosophy*. These translations helped to improve the underdeveloped English prose of that period and contributed to the improvement of the English language as a whole.

In the 12th and 13th centuries, the Toledo School of Translators, also known as the Escuela de Traductores de Toledo, became a gathering place for intellectuals from all over Europe. These intellectuals were drawn to Toledo, Spain, by the high wages offered, and they settled there to translate important philosophical, religious, scientific, and medical works from Arabic, Greek, and Hebrew into Latin and Castilian. It was one of the few locations in medieval Europe during which a Christian might be introduced to Arabic culture and language since Toledo was a city of institutions that offered a lot of different manuscripts. Toledo was also known for its rich history.

The Toledo Academy of Translators dominated discussions on translation activities in the 5th century. There are two phases that may be distinguished in the history of the Toledo Academy of Translators.

Archbishop Raymond de Toledo, who headed the movement during the first era (which occurred in the 12th century), is credited with promoting the translation of philosophical and theological texts, "mostly from classical Arabic into Latin" (Mohandas, 2008). These Latin translations contributed to the development of scholasticism in Europe, which advanced "European science and culture" (Holmes, 2000). During the second phase, which occurred in the 13th century, "King Alfonso X of Castile" (House, 2011) was in charge. The academics also translated works in science and medicine in addition to the philosophical and theological texts they were responsible for. Castilian, not Latin, is the language that ultimately prevailed, and as a consequence, the foundations of the contemporary Spanish language were laid using this language.

The translations of works on various sciences (astronomy, astrology, algebra, and medicine), "acted as a magnet for numerous scholars, who came from all over Europe to Toledo to learn firsthand about the contents of all those Arabic", Greek, and Hebrew works, before going back home to disseminate the knowledge acquired in European universities (Sawant 2013, p.28). These scholars translated works on astronomy, astrology, algebra, and medicine. At the same time as specific Toledo translations of scientific and cosmological writings were approved at most "European institutions in the early 1200s, the works of Aristotle and Arab thinkers were often forbidden", as was the case at the Sorbonne University in Paris.

Roger Bacon was an English scholar who lived in the 13th century and is credited with being the first person to provide a "universal grammar". He was the first linguist to determine that in "order to produce a good translation" (Baker and Saldanha, 2009), a translator needed to have a strong command of both the language from which the text was taken and the language into which it was to be rendered. In addition, the translator needed a solid foundation in the subject matter of his work. The story goes that when Roger Bacon saw that very few translators understood what he was saying, he "decided to do away with translation and translators completely" (Delisle and Woodsworth, 2012). However, he did not stick with his choice for very long. He depended heavily on Toledo's translations from Arabic into Latin to contribute significantly to optics, astronomy, chemistry, and mathematics disciplines. Toledo was responsible for many of the translations.

Geoffrey Chaucer is credited with producing the first high-quality translations into English somewhere in the 14th century. The "Roman de la Rose" and Boethius's writings were initially written in French before being translated into English by Chaucer. In addition to this, he rewrote some of the "works of the Italian humanist Giovanni Boccaccio" and published them in English under the titles "Knight's Tale" and "Troilus and Criseyde" around the year 1385 (Gentzler, 2010). It is generally accepted that Chaucer was the originator of the English poetry tradition that was "based on translations and adaptations of literary works" originally written in languages that were considered to be "more established" than English at the time, starting with Latin and Italian. "Wycliffe's Bible" (1382-84), which was named "after John Wycliffe, an English theologian who translated the Bible from Latin to English", is considered to be the best religious translation that was produced during that period.

Gemistus Pletho, a scholar from Byzantium, on a voyage to Florence, Italy, considered the beginning of the rebirth of Greek scholarship in Western Europe. Plato's ideas were reintroduced by Gemistus Pletho at the Council of Florence in 1438-39 in an effort that was ultimately unsuccessful in reconciling the East-West division. Pletho convinced Cosimo de Medici to establish a Platonic Academy via their conversation. The Latin translation of all of Plato's works, including the *Enneads* of Plotinus and other Neoplatonist writings, was taken up by the Platonic Academy, which was "led by the Italian scholar and translator Marsilio Ficino". The work of Marsilio Ficino and Erasmus' Latin version of the New Testament contributed to the development of a fresh perspective on translation. Readers, for the first time, required a rigorous interpretation of the text since their philosophical and theological convictions were dependent on the precise "words of Plato and Jesus (and Aristotle and others)" (Sawant, 2013, p.23).

2.4. Translation in the 16th Century

The advent of publishing media, and the shift away from Latin in the 1400s and 1500s, led to the creation of the inaugural multilingual printing business, of which various translation initiatives remain. As the publishing industry expanded to include works in other languages, the Bible in Martin Luther's German translation from Latin appeared in print for the first time. Martin Luther thought the Bible needed to be translated so ordinary Germans and intellectuals could read it. Bible translation into modern languages began in earnest in the 1500s. During this time, the Bible became one of the most notable reproduced books in history, and its many variants significantly impacted the development of European languages.

The 16th century saw a significant shift in translation practices not limited to the Bible's adaptation. Since 1598, George Chapman authored his translation of the *Iliad* in installments, and in 1616, the complete *Iliad* and *Odyssey* surfaced in *The Full Writings of Homer*, "the first English translation" (House, 2011), was the most prominent in the English language and served as the way that so many English speakers experienced these writings. John Keats had a great deal of admiration for this individual's translation of Homer. In addition, Chapman was responsible for the translation of the *Homeric Hymns*, the *Georgics* by Vergil, the compositions of Hesiod (1618, which were dedicated to Francis Bacon), the *Hero and Leander* by Musaeus (1618), and the fifth Satire of Juvenal (1624).

Since its first publication in folio in 1614–16, Chapman's translation of Homer's epic poem the *Odyssey*, which was first released in 1614–16, has become so scarce that it is inaccessible to the typical reader and relatively obscure to the more inquisitive students of ancient English literature (translation). Martin Luther (1483-1546) had already printed "his German translation of the New Testament in 1522". He and his colleagues had finished the translation of the Old Testament in 1534, at which point the whole work was published. He worked until the last moment of his lifetime to perfect the translation into English. Several people had already translated the Bible into German before Luther, but he was the first to personalize it according to his ideology. Luther's translation was done in German, which was understandable to people from both the north and the south of Germany since it was the German used at the Saxon Chancellery. The Luther Bible contributed substantially to the development of "German language and literature," in addition to the field of translation.

The practice of translation was further expanded throughout the 16th century as a result of an increase in the need for fresh literary material on a worldwide scale, as well as an extension of the publishing procedure and the development of the academic middle class during that same period. During this period, "William Tyndale", a well-known English scholar in the year 1525, was in charge of leading a group of people who were working on the "first Tudor translation of the New Testament" (Sawant, 2013, p.19). The texts in Hebrew and Greek have been directly translated into English for the first time. This particular portion of the Bible was among the first to go through this process. After he finished translating the New Testament, Tyndale set his sights on translating the first portion of the "Old Testament." He was successful in doing so.

Furthermore, as Baker and Saldanha (2009, p.49) stated, "Martin Luther, a German professor of theology," who lived during this period, played a pivotal role in the Protestant Reformation, and later in his life, he also translated the Bible into German. He was the earliest European to make the daring assertion that one can only translate correctly towards his original language, a remark that would become the accepted standard two centuries after he made it. The printing and distribution of the "Luther Bible" were essential in the evolution of the current common German language.

In addition to the "Luther Bible" in German, which was published between 1522 and 1534, two additional significant translations were the "Jakub Wujek Bible" ("Biblia Jakuba Wujka") in Polish, which was published in 1535, and the "King James Bible" in English, which was published between 1604 and 1611. All three of these translations had a long-lasting impact on Germany, Poland, and England's religion, language, and culture. These translations exhibited discrepancies in critical terms and sentences, which led, to some degree, to the division of "Western Christianity into Roman Catholicism and Protestantism." This happened on top of the purpose of the Protestant Reformation to eradicate corruption in the Roman Catholic Church.

In addition to these languages, "the Bible was rendered into Dutch, French, Spanish, Czech, and Slovene." Jacob van Lisevelt was the first to print the Bible in Dutch in 1526. Jacques Lefevre d'Étaples is credited as being the first person to "print the Bible in French" in the year 1528. Casiodoro de Reina was the first to print the Scripture in Spanish in 1569 under the title "Biblia del Oso." In 1584, a translation of the Bible into Slovene was made available to the public by Jurij Dalmatian. Between 1579 and 1593, many editions of the Bible, also known as the "Bible kralická," were published. Christian Europeans' translations of the Bible were a motivating force in the usage of local dialects, leading to the formation of all of the modern languages used in Europe today.

2.5. Translation in the 17th Century

The golden period of French classicism was the 17th century. From 1625 to 1660, there was a flourishing translation of French classics into other languages, including English. According to Sir John Denham's perspective, the translator and the original author are on the same footing, with the only distinctions being those of society and time.

In the "Preface" to his translation of Pindar's Odes, Abraham Cowley argued for the right of artistic license and recognized imitation as a distinct kind of translation. John Dryden spent most of his final twenty years revising and translating works from antiquity. In the 18th century, practically all discussions of translation began with his prologue to Ovid's Epistles.

Also, several essential theorists were born in the 17th century, such as Sir John Denham (1615–169), Abraham Cowley (1618–67), John Dryden (1631–1700), who is best known for differentiating between metaphrase, paraphrase, and imitation in translation, and Alexander Pope (1688-1744). As opposed to writing for the theatre, Dryden found more fulfillment in translating the works of Horace, Juvenal, Ovid, Lucretius, and Theocritus. His magnum opus and distinguishing works in translation, *The Works of Vergil* (1697) was a subscription publication that he started working on in 1694.

Nicolas Perrot d'Ablancourt was a modern French translator of the Greek and Latin classics, and he said that his translations "remind me of a lady whom I passionately loved in Tours, who was lovely but unfaithful" (Amaro Hurtado Albir, "La concept de fidélité en traduction," Didier Érudition, 1990). By making stylistic changes to the original text, Perrot d'Ablancourt was following the controversial practice of Valentin Conrart, a French author and founder of the Académie Française. Additional French writers, including Huygens and Voltaire, popularised the phrase "belle infidèle" after its introduction by Flaubert.

It was not until the latter part of the 17th century that the concepts of "faithfulness" and "transparency" were separated from one another as distinct, sometimes conflicting goals. "Faithfulness" refers to how well a translation stays true to the original text in terms of content, style, and tone while also considering the work's topic, purpose, audience, and other factors. A translation is said to be "transparent" if it gives the impression to "a native speaker of the target language" (Sawant 2013, p.20) that it was written in that language, using its grammar, syntax, and idioms. "Idiomatic" is often used to describe a "transparent" translation.

2.6. Translation in the 18th Century

Over the years, translators' commitment to precision has become an industry standard. Accuracy, style, and policy in translation were the cornerstones of the first stage of the industrial revolution. This may have started during the Victorian period when translators felt obligated to inform their audiences that the works they were admiring had been initially written in a language other than their own. This necessitated the use of footnotes to provide further context.

In the 18th century, translators were seen as professional artists who had a fiduciary responsibility to both the creator of the source text and the reader of the translated version. In addition, the development of new ideas and monographs on the translation process facilitated the methodical study of translation; one such example is Alexander Fraser Tytler's *Principles of Translation* (1791). Authors like George Campbell and Samuel Johnson are prominent figures from this period. The work by Tytler is significant in the development of translation theory. He argued that a good translation would be faithful to the original in terms of content and style and would also have the natural flow of the source text. At the turn of the century, translators began prioritizing readability. The parts of the text they did not grasp or found uninteresting were eliminated. This century ended with "the British East India imperial administration" (Venuti, 2008) taking a keen interest in their subjects' languages, literature, and culture; as a result, the discovery and translation of old Indian works were actively promoted. Scholars from the 18th century believed that translators should keep modern readers in mind while working on a new translation and that this would result in a more faithful representation of the original author's intent and style.

In this century, the translation strategy is based on the text, with a strong emphasis on style and precision. Since this is set in the Victorian period, crude language is acceptable. It was also decided that there should be some footnoted explanations. Translators tried to alert readers that their works were adaptations from other languages. Edward FitzGerald's rendition of the *Rubaiyat of Omar Khayyám* is another deviation from the norm. Surprisingly, notwithstanding the accessibility of increasingly comprehensive and modern translations of the poetry, his versions remain the most renowned.

2.7. Translation in the 19th Century

The 19th century was characterized by two opposing inclinations: the first saw translation as a classification of consciousness and viewed the translators as resourceful geniuses who enhance the literary works and vocabulary into what they translate, whereas the other one saw translation through the functional purpose of creating a content or a writer widely recognized. This time frame also saw the rise of Romanticism, a fact that paved the way for the development of a significant number of ideas and translations in the field of literature, most notably poetic translation. This translation was utilized by Edward Fitzgerald (1809-63) for *Rubaiyat Omar Al-Khayyam*, and it is an excellent example of the translation (1858). Percy Bysshe Shelley (1792-1822), often considered one of the most influential poets in Western culture, was also an accomplished translator. He was responsible for the translation of three of Plato's dialogues, the first of which was the *Symposium* (The Banquet) in 1818, followed by *Ion* in 1821. However, the Phaedo translation that he worked on is no longer available. Shelley's translation is a far better vehicle for Plato's work than the somewhat chatty and colloquial translations that are common at this time because of the elevated and sophisticated nature of Shelley's style.

In 1821, prominent author, critic, and poet Samuel Taylor Coleridge (1772-1834) translated an essential piece of literature titled *Faust* by Goethe. Dante Gabriel Rossetti (1828-1882) spent a significant portion of his life working "on English translations of Italian poetry." These translations included Dante Alighieri's *La Vita Nuova* and were eventually collected and presented as the Early Italian Poets in 1861, where his primary focus was. Because of this, the 19th century was characterized by a proliferation of translations into English from a wide range of languages, such as the translation of Goethe's works from German into English and the translation of the *Rubaiyat of Omar Khayyam*, which is a collection of poems, from Persian into English. Both of these works were published in the United Kingdom. In addition to being translated into a plethora of languages throughout the globe, "the Bible was also translated into numerous Indian languages," and many books and materials written initially in English were also translated into Indian languages. It is important to note that vocabulary listings, including linguistic characteristics of the languages spoken by people living in European colonies, were developed. These were subsequently used to make translating the Bible more accessible.

In his discussion of the activities related to the translation that took place throughout the 19th century, Newmark (1988) hypothesized that the area of translation experienced a proliferation of bizarre notions during that period. Shelley had a cynical attitude towards translation, whereas Coleridge made an effort to differentiate between fancy and imagination. Fredrich Schleiermacher proposed that a distinct sublanguage be used for translation and that this sublanguage should demonstrate integrity to the structures and vocabulary of the source. The literal interpretation, Victorian-era archaism, and formalist approach were all emphasized in this translation. In contrast to Dryden and Pope, the Victorians were interested in demonstrating the historical and geographical distance between their version and the original. For instance, "Mathew Arnold's translation of Homer into English" was criticized for being too literal and failing to capture the essence of the poet's work as it was originally written. These "Revised and American Standard Versions" of the Bible are the clearest examples of the damage that may be done by a translation that is too literalistic and was done in the Victorian period.

The method of Bible translation also worked until the early 1800s, just before early industrialization introduced new challenges. As industrial production began during the Industrial Revolution of the 19th century in the United States and Europe, so did the demand for accurate records. This needs to be translated into a language that could be used to sell in international markets.

2.8. Translation in the 20th Century

As we moved into the 20th century, the translation business got more
organized, and technological advancements occurred rapidly. During this
century, translation theories emerged, and it became vital to convey the
intended meaning rather than only the words themselves. That time saw the
birth of what is now often called "Translation Studies", an academic field
dedicated to the study of translation. Traditional translation and translation
studies have also persisted from the turn of the century until the 1990s.

In the 20th century, religious and political forces considered translation
a social activity. As a result, numerous groups and organizations were
founded and encouraged the translation of the Bible into a wide variety of
languages, including the languages spoken by primitive and tribal
communities. Toward the end of the 20th century, precision and literary
quality became translation considerations. Translations were seen as a
political mission in the political arena of this century, and highly political
material was "translated into English from Chinese, Russian, and other
Asian and European languages," as well as from Canadian and French into
English and vice versa. It is essential to highlight that the translation of
sexual and religious material in China started in the 1980s and was warmly
appreciated, despite this practice being discouraged throughout the
"Cultural Revolution". During the same era, research on translation
developed as an essential subject for students to study while they were in
school to learn a language. In addition, it led to the creation of products for
translation research, such as computerized translation (also known as CAT)
tools and machine translation.

The middle part of the 20th century witnessed the introduction of a new
academic field known as "Translation Studies", as well as the establishment
of new institutions that specialized in teaching said field. James S. Holmes,
a poet as well as a translator of poetry, is credited with coining the name
"Translation Studies" in his landmark work "The Name and Nature of
Translation Studies" (1972). This publication is considered the fundamental
declaration for this newly established academic field. Despite being
established in the US, Holmes spent most of his childhood in Amsterdam,
in the Netherlands. While composing his poems, he translated several
Belgian and Dutch poets' works into English. In 1964, the University of
Amsterdam established a separate "Institute of Translators and Translators",
which has since been renamed the Institute of Translation Studies. He was
employed as an associate professor there and went on to write a number of
influential publications on the subject of translation.

From antiquity until the middle of the 20th century, translating was considered a specialized type of spoken translation instead of written translation. Only later did translating become its distinct field of study. Translating Studies progressively emancipated themselves from Translation Studies to focus on the pragmatic and educational aspects of translating and create a particular multidisciplinary conceptual model. This model provides cultural and social investigations of translation services and their working environment, which is still sorely lacking in sociological studies of translators and their working conditions.

2.9. Translation in the 21st Century

Access to translation was revolutionized with the advent of the internet and the development of reliable online translation tools in the 21st century. The need for communicating across cultures grew rapidly, and the introduction of Google Translate in 2006 made it possible for anybody with access to the web to translate text easily. Neural machine translation (NMT) has been the center of attention for the last several years, and it has already revolutionized the language sector, with Google Translate announcing its transition to NMT in 2016.

Modern translators have made significant contributions to the development of the languages they have worked with. As a result, the target language has been enriched by including words previously unavailable in the target language but present in the original language. Calques (words or phrases taken from another language via direct translation) and loanwords (words accepted from a language and absorbed into another without translation) from the source language have enhanced the target languages through spillovers of idiom and use.

The historical agency of translators is defended by Venuti (2008) in *The Translator's Invisibility: A History of Translation*. He illustrates how translations have altered the Western literary canon, influenced the development of academic and scholarly thinking across time, and shaped how people see other cultures. He contends that translators need to rethink their position, away from the usual domestication of translations toward a more open acceptance of the infiltration of foreign influences into translated writings. Translation experts have had much to say about his work, which has become the standard reference library for its domain.

There is a need for translators to choose a specialty (legal, economic, technical, scientific, literary) to be trained appropriately. A global market for translators, language localizers, and translation tools has emerged because of the proliferation of online communication. An upsurge of unwaged voluntary translations (including crowd-sourcing translations) promulgated by large organizations with the resources to hire many professionals, but no professional translators, has also brought many challenges for translators, including lower fees, insecure employment and a dearth of freelance work that pays the bills.

To succeed as a translator, bilingual speakers need more to offer than just a command of two languages. A professional translator requires fluency in two languages and an expert-level understanding of one subject. This was self-evident during the Medieval Era and the centuries that followed, but it is less so nowadays. Numerous translation experts have become "invisible" in the 21st century, despite having been recognized as intellectuals alongside writers and academics for two millennia. Their names are no longer included in press releases or on the covers of the books and articles they labored over for days, weeks, or months.

Despite the prevalence of MT (machine translation) and CAT (computer-assisted translation) technologies that are meant to speed up the translation process, some translators nonetheless want to be likened to artists... and not only because of the precarious nature of their working conditions. In *The Translator's Endless Toil*, Christopher Kasparek (1983) argues that a literary translator's job is to "interpret" a book in the same way that a musician or actor would. Some translators who aren't writers nonetheless strive for the status of "artist" in their field because of the skill, expertise, devotion, and enthusiasm they bring to their job.

Works cited

Baker, M., and Saldanha, G (2009) Routledge Encyclopedia of Translation Studies, London: Routledge.

Delisle, J. and J. Woodsworth (eds.) (1995) Translators through History, Amsterdam and Philadelphia, PA: John Benjamins.

Gentzler, E. (2010) Contemporary Translation Theory. New Delhi: Viva Books.

Holmes, J. S. (2000) "The name and nature of translation studies", in The Translation Studies Reader, L. Venuti (ed.) London: Routledge. pp. 180–92.

House, J. (2011) A Model for Translation Quality Assessment: A Model Revisited, Tubingen: Gunten Narr.

Mohanda, T. S. T. (2008) Text-Wise in Translation. Malaysia: Prentice Hall.

Newmark, P. (1988) A Textbook of Translation. New York and London: Prentice-Hall.

Nida, E. A and C. R. Taber (1969) The Theory and Practice of Translation, Leiden: E. J. Bill.

Saldanha, G. (2009) Research Methodologies in Translation Studies. Abingdon: Routledge.

Sawanti, H. (2013) History of translation. International Journal of Language and Translation Studies.

Venuti, L. (ed.) (2004). The Translation Studies Reader. USA and Canada: Routledge.

CHAPTER THREE

EXPLORING THE THEORIES OF TRANSLATION

3.1 Introduction to Theories of Translation

It is a prevalent practice to establish the explanation of various fields of study from diverse theoretical points of view. The evolution of theories will always be an essential part of the narrative of such a field from its beginnings to its present state. Many researchers have established theoretical perspectives for translation study and actual actions in translation because translation is considered one of the oldest fields of inquiry. The primary purpose of theories of translation is to identify acceptable procedures of translation for the broadest possible variety of materials or text categories. In addition to this, it provides a foundation for problem-solving as well as the development of a conceptual model that includes rules, constraints, and pointers for evaluating translations and materials that have been translated. Every theory worthy of consideration needs to center its attention on the translation procedures used to solve the challenges and difficulties brought about by particular materials. Closely to this, Munday (2008) contends that any schools of thought built on translation perspectives need to generally incorporate formal study into the fundamental prerequisites for translation and that this is a precondition for any critical theory of translation.

It is essential to draw a contrast between the terms "translation theory" and "theories of translation" to emphasize the difference between the two. The former is a chronological transformation of translation as anthropogenic activity, from a practical act of translating texts to a theoretical activity of studying the fundamentals of translation from a broad range of perspectives. In contrast, the latter encompasses a formulated conceptual model for the practical translation and survey of translation through certain viewpoints. In other words, the latter entails a developed framework for the practical translation and study of translation through particular perspectives. Translation theory is the discipline that sparked the interest and ambition that led to the formation of theories of translation.

According to Munday and Zhang (2015), the growth of translation theory has hastened the acknowledgment of two separate dimensions in translation studies. The first aspect is the acknowledgment of translation status as a purely theoretical endeavor, with the role of translation researchers limited to speculating on the many meanings conveyed by the act. The second aspect is the awareness of translation as an operational commitment, in which the exclusive emphasis of translators is on producing equal texts in the target language for materials written in the source language. The theoretical activities in translation as a theory have provided practical translators with specific and generic directions, methods, strategies, and techniques for providing suitable equivalents in the target language. These have been made available due to the theoretical activities in translation as a theory.

Another aspect that has played a role in the development of theories of translation is the need to satisfy specific contextual criteria in translation. This is one of the reasons why theories of translation were developed. Recent advancements in translation have resulted in a change in emphasis away from the preservation of the original text in the source language and toward the provision of equivalents that cater to the urgent communication requirements of the intended audience. In addition, some theories have been established to fulfill the requirements of translation in specific fields, such as legal documents.

Considerably, there are arrays of studies in translation that have amounted to the development of theories of translation. To proceed, it is essential to talk about the various theories of translation, mentioning where the theories came from or how they evolved, the assumptions of the theories, methods, or translation techniques that have been created as a result of these theories, and exploring specific criticisms of the theories.

3.2. Perspectival Directions in Translation Theories

Attempts to study theories of translation have yielded three main perspectival directions, including:

i.   Theories of translation from a historical or chronological perspective.
ii. Theories of translation from individual's schools of thought.
iii. Theories of translation from a locational perspective.

Arguably, there are more perspectives that can form a bloc in the discussion of theories of translation. However, these three perspectival directions underpin the discussion of theories of translation in this textbook.

3.3. Theories of Translation from a Historical or Chronological Perspectives

After a comprehensive search, it became clear that several translation theories had been formulated throughout the development and early phases of the translation process. Diverse schools of thought in translation at various times have developed these theories, primarily focusing on issues of equivalence, reliability of the source language message during translation into the second language, current concerns in the requirements of the target language audience, and quality depletion. The following theories of translation have developed throughout time:

1. The philological theory
2. The linguistic theory
3. The functional dimension in translation

3.3.1. The Philological Theories

Philology, which encompasses the investigation of and evaluation of textual components, primarily underlying inventiveness, configuration, connotation, and symbolic meanings, has served as the predominant framework for analyzing translation practices for more than five centuries (Robinson, 1997). This has been the case throughout the entire field. As a result, at the time, these works looked to be the only writings that deserved to be translated into other languages; these kinds of jobs were considered literary productions.

Philological ideas are dependent on philosophy and history, which is the investigation of the development of language in addition to the studying of literary texts. Comparing the language forms of the target language and the source language, specifically the organizational relationship and the textual styles, in combination with translation criticism and ideology, is the central objective of philologists who work in the field of translation. This is done by drawing parallels between the two sets of language's grammatical structures. The substance of literature has served as the basis for the philological approach to the translation process. The basics of this translation evaluation method are being used in imagery studies as part of the ongoing translation study, and it is also being extended to cover literary translation analyses.

Philological techniques for translation tackle the problem of equivalence between different literary works by conducting an in-depth comparison and contrast of the source language (SL) and the target language (TL). In addition, they focus on the literary quality of the article, paying special consideration to the form of the content, its aesthetic attributes, and persuasive methods. Another critical difficulty that arises in philological theories of translation is the question of whether or not literary genres in the target and source languages are equivalent to one another. One of the critical concerns of these ideas was determining if poems must be translated into prose or vice versa, including if an epic in the source language ought to be rendered in the target language in its original form.

As Nida and Taber (1969) stated, philological notions of translation are based on a philological approach to literary study. This is true for every single philological theory out there. They essentially take things an additional step forward by, instead of analyzing the pattern within which the text was initially created, concentrating on comparable forms between the original language as well as the target language and striving to assess to what extent to which these forms are comparable to one another. This is done to determine whether or not the text has been successfully translated. In general, philological theories of translation are associated with a diverse range of rhetorical methods and stylistic characteristics.

This theoretical dimension does not immediately give rise to any translation techniques; rather, it is regarded as an approach, a theory, and a method. There are no translation methods that arose directly from this theoretical dimension. The philological perspective of translation has developed as a technique and principle that govern the translation of literary works, as stated by Kim, Munday, Wang, and Wang (2021).

3.3.2. Linguistic Theory of Translation

Boase-Beier (2010) states that the linguistic theory of translation is based on contrasting the grammatical structures of the source material and TL text rather than evaluating writing styles and artistic characteristics. These ideas emerged due to the dizzying growth of modern linguistic theory and the trend toward more applied linguistics. There is a school of thought among linguists and translation theorists that holds that "translation theory is an aspect of semantics; all issues of semantics belong to translation theory" (Marais, 2018, p.23). In contrast to philological theories of translation, linguistic theories of translation, as argued by Newmark (1981), concentrate on characterization instead of prescribing. Munday (2012) argues that these theories show not how translation should be done but how people do it. According to Nida and Taber (1969), the main difference between the various models of translation and semi-theories is in whether they prioritize similar surface structures or analogous deep structures. Connecting the surface and the underlying shapes may help distill many concepts to their essence. These evaluations often come with elaborate standards for picking the best possible pair.

Since there are often different languages concerned in a translation, it's unsurprising that some researchers studying translation problems have zeroed down on the differences between them. Instead of just translating statements word-for-word, translators have always prioritized creating connections between words that indicate something. In addition, the linguistic theory of translation suggests that although it is helpful to zero in on processes, it is also vital to think about the text's original context and any functional aspects that could be lost in translation. This progress has been a big help in the quest for a less naïve phenomenology in translation theory.

According to Levy (2011), linguistic theories of translation are where we get the ideas behind translation methods like literal translation, trans-definition, trans-literation, calque, and other approaches and techniques that focus on the structure of a language. All the methodologies that have emerged from this perspective center on the organization of the original text and the best ways to preserve that structure and the original meaning in the translated text.

3.3.3. The Functionalist Theory of Translation

The functionalist or communicative approach to the translation study emerged in Germany during the 1970s and 1980s, signifying a break from the previous rigid linguistic categorizations of translation. The theory of translation operations, the skopos theory (Baker, 2005, pp.235-238; Shuttleworth and Cowie, 2007, pp.156-157), and the theory of text analysis are all examples of these philosophies.

In response to traditional linguistic translation research, Katharina Reib and Hans J. Vermeer developed the functional translation theory. The two academics realized that the new method's paradigms needed a new language, so they set out to create the functionalist theory of translation. Beyond the scope of James S. Holmes's "The Name and Nature of Translation Studies", the authors argue that their method has far-reaching implications (1985). Terms like "target" and "source" language, "text," "author," and "reader" were often employed in the past. However, terminology like "receptor text," "source text," and "receptor" has become increasingly commonplace in recent years. The translator is the protagonist, and the translated text is the setting since translation is seen as a method.

The premise of this new idea is that language and culture are inextricably linked and reinforce one another. Functionalist theories of translation challenge the role of the translator as an intermediary by recasting the translator as an independent text creator who shapes a new text according to the needs of the target audience.

The Skopos model of translation is only one of several theories and sub-theories that have emerged from this approach.

The Skopos assumption has become one of the most critical functionalist translation hypotheses. Various researchers have adapted the concepts of this model to the task of translating texts that, rather than faithfully preserving the original content, attempt to communicate it to intended users. This line of thinking maintains that the principles of action may include the ideas of translations as communication across cultures since contents are developed with a particular primary objective and participant in mind. Consequently, translation practice is a distinct subset of the communication arts. The first step in this process is creating an original writing piece. These words are the springboard for this activity. Translators should not worry about whether or not to take action but rather about what information to transmit and how to proceed. If seen from this perspective, theories of the translation may be appreciated for what they are: complex theories of action. The Greek term skopos is equivalent to the English phrases "purpose", "goal", and "function". Even if the translated text's Skopos differs from the source text (a shift in intent), the translated text and its outputs must be consistent.

The Skopos Theory upholds that the translated "translatum" does not have to have the same meaning as the original text to be regarded as a valid translation. Skopos theory places greater weight on the target culture than the source culture, yet both are studied in depth. One of Vermeer's definitions of an "intercultural activity" is a request for translation. As a result, the translator must determine the final purpose of the translated text (Green, 2012, p.109). In this context, Vermeer defines a translation brief as an "order, either by oneself or by someone else, to carry out a specific duty, in this case: "to translate." As Jensen (2009) points out, a translation brief, on the other hand, may or may not be explicitly expressed (in response to a client's request) (Nord, 2006), and it may be communicated either verbally or in writing (Jensen, 2009). However, the Skopos concept needs a translation brief to instruct the translators (Green, 2012).

Several concerns have been raised about bringing Skopos theory into the study of translation. Skopos theory has been criticized by those who concentrate on language for a number of reasons, including the basic overgeneralization of functionalist methods, the privileging of the text over the plethora of interpretations, and the impediment to the authority of SL text. These objections stem from the skopos theory's narrow emphasis on the message at the expense of nuance (Baker, 2005, p.237). This strategy is contested because even if a translation succeeds in expressing the original text's Skopos, it may be criticized for other reasons, such as the translation's lexical, syntactic, or aesthetic choices at the sentence level.

3.4. Theories of Translation from Individual Schools of Thought

Various individuals throughout the history of translation have developed different schools of thought or theoretical projections that have emerged as perspectives in the contemporary study of translation. These schools of thought and theoretical projections are known as perspectives. Some of these academics are also responsible for the nomenclature of the theories that they have produced, as can be seen in the list below:

i. The theory of translation developed by Dryden
ii. The theory of translation developed by Catford
iii. The Theory of Translation Proposed by Nida
iv. The theory of translation developed by Susan Bassenet and Andre Levefre
v. The translation theory proposed by Venuti

At different points in the course of the history of translation, these academics were in the spotlight as the primary topic of conversation at the international level. They have established themselves as an authority and have become focal points in the ongoing debate on translation ideas. Their perspectives on translation are investigated further in the parts discussed below.

3.4.1. Dryden's Theory of Translation

Dryden's work was a continuation of the views that Chapman, d'Ablancourt, and Denham had provided before. However, the limited hypotheses provided by the thinker during this period were primarily rooted in the historical perspectives of Horace and Cicero. They have not made many new contributions or advancements in those already established ideas. The theory translation gained both a new face and fresh impetus as a result of the introduction of Dryden. He made extensive contributions to the theory of translation. Dryden was known for his work in the literary genres of poetry and theatre. Ancient works such as Ovid's Epistles (1680) discussed the three different translation styles in the prefaces that he wrote for his translations of classics, most notably the one he wrote for Ovid's Epistles (1680). He summarised all translations by grouping them under these three categories: 1. Metaphrase; 2. Paraphrase; and 3. Imitation, (Venuti, 2021).

1. The term "metaphrase" refers to the process of translating the work of an author literally "word for word and line by line" into another language.
2. The term "paraphrase" refers to a kind of translation that incorporates flexibility.
3. The term "imitation" refers to the act of presenting and rewriting the material in accordance with his preferences.

The second group, which Dryden referred to as "Paraphrase", was his favourite. Dryden drew parallels between the work of a translator and that of a portrait painter because a portrait painter is expected to create a portrait similar to the actual subject being portrayed.

3.4.2. Catford's Theory of Translation

Catford examines the nature of translation and proposes a theory about it in his work titled "A Linguistic Theory of Translation". His approach might be described as analytical. First, he talks about "language", and then he describes his concept of translation. According to him, the practice of translating is a process that is carried out in two distinct languages. According to his perspective, language is:

1. The manner in which people engage with one another in a social setting.
2. An activity connected to natural occurrences and vocal motions.

He worked on the assumption that translation can be done between any two languages, regardless of whether they are related or not. He defines translation as the substitution of literary content in one language (SL) with similarly written texts in another language (TL). In his definition, Catford makes use of two crucial terms: equivalent, as well as textual substance.

According to Catford, finding a translation equivalent in the target language is the most critical challenge facing translators today. He offers many general kinds of translation regarding the size, degrees, and rankings involved.

Catford offered the following forms of translation based on this theoretical approach to translation:

i.   When the whole text in SL is replaced with its equivalent in TL, he refers to this as a complete translation.

ii. On the other hand, if during the process of translation, any portion of the source text does not be translated but is nonetheless included in the target language, this is known as a partial translation. Items are sometimes utilised on purpose as they are for the sole purpose of adding local flavour.

iii. He believes the phrase "complete translation" is deceptive since it refers to translating a source language text into a target language text at all levels. It is a term that refers to the incorporation of SL grammar, lexis, and graphology into TL writing.

iv. A translation is said to be restricted if, at any level, the source language (SL) text is changed to the target language (TL) text. Phonological or graphological analysis might be done at this level. Even limited translation refers to replacing SL grammar with TL grammar but without replacing TL lexis and TL lexis with TL lexis without replacing TL grammar. However, restricted translation does not include replacing TL lexis with TL grammar.

v.   The rank bound translation is the process of translating between texts that have the same rank in the source language and the target language, such as sentence to sentence, word to word, or group to group.

vi. The term "free translation" is sometimes used to refer to unbounded translation, a kind of translation in which counterparts may move freely across levels.

Catford expressed an interest in investigating the possibilities. Catford focuses on the procedures and tactics that a translator should adopt at the phonological, grammatical, and syntactic levels when he is explaining his ideas of translation from the perspective of language considerations. This is done so in order to illuminate his theories of translation. He also describes how "rank changes" may be achieved via translation, while maintaining his primary point that there may be no one-to-one relationship among any multiple categories in the foreground of his mind at all times.

a) A change within a single tier for occurrences in the meaning itself when translating notions such as bravery and chastity, which differ from one culture to another and throughout the course of history.

b) Move through one layer to the other, such as from the syntactic level to the morphemic level. According to Catford's argument, in order for a translator to convey what the original author said in a single morpheme, the original author's meaning must be articulated in a whole sentence.

3.4.3. Nida's Theory of Translation

Eugene Nida was a scholar of languages. He started his professional life working for the "American Bible Society (ABS)". Up to his retirement, he served as the Associate Secretary for Translation. His views are mainly based on his challenges while working on the Bible translation. When he was developing his theory of translation, Nida took into consideration linguistics, semantics, communication theory, and anthropology. As a result, his theory is the most complete one. The communicative approach to meaning is given significant weight in Nida's (1978) *Toward a Science of Translating*. The communicative frame, which is an essential component of his theory, is provided by him. After making a reference to a typical monolingual communication scenario, he goes on to say that translation is an "interlingual act". He then offers an example. He saw the process of translation as a convoluted kind of communication that consisted of two distinct phases: the encoding phase and the decoding phase.

Culture has a significant influence on the process of communication that is taking place here. Both the person who is sending and receiving the communication come from the same cultural background. According to Nida (1969), "Translation is not a process of matching surface forms by rules of correspondence but rather a more complicated method including analysis, transfer, and restructure." Eugene Nida's contribution to linguistics was significant due to the ideas he developed on translation; in particular, his concept of the dynamical and functional equivalency is outstanding. In addition, he devised a novel approach to the pursuit of equivalence. The term for this methodology is "componential analysis." It advises breaking down words into their constituent parts in order to assist in determining equivalency in translation (for example, "bachelor" might be translated as "male" and "unmarried"). When discussing the differences between the two versions, Nida took into account the following three fundamental aspects:

1. The Characteristics of the Message

2. The objective of the author and the translator
3. The demographics of the audience

Since he claimed that there is nothing that can be referred to as an identical equivalent, he proposed a different word, which he dubbed the "closest natural equivalence". He is of the opinion that no translation may be an exact counterpart of its original, and the reason for this is because he believes all forms of translation entail the following:

i.   Loss of knowledge
ii. The creation of new information
iii. The manipulation of existing information

According to Nida, the process of translation consists of three stages: analysis, transfer, and reconstruction. In the first step of the analysis, he takes into account the grammatical connection between the constituent elements, the contextual interpretations of the conceptual components, as well as the referential elements of the sentence rules and the semantic units. The studied text from the source language (SL) is then translated into the target language (TL) in the translator's mind during the second transfer stage. The final and last part of the Restructuring process involves reconstructing the material that was transferred into the TL. Even though Nida's theory is based on language, he recognises the significance of the role played by culture. According to him, the process of translation is a kind of communication that is much more complicated than others since it involves alternating stages as decode and encoding. Equivalence is widely regarded as one of the most essential core words in the field of translation theories. This phrase has been the source of a great deal of debate. Dynamic equivalence, also known as Functional Equivalence, is a theory developed by Eugene Nida that emphasises the significance of transmitting meaning rather than grammatical structure. He spoke on the concept of translation as well as its many different difficulties. Nida asserts in his work titled *The Theory and Practice of Translation* that the translators of the Bible were not successful in communicating its central message. He remarked that there were two alternative ways of approaching the problem, which recommended two different translation strategies. The form was given a significant amount of weight in the previous approach. They attempted a reproduction in terms of style, but the new method placed a greater emphasis on the recipient's reaction. The concept of formal equivalence focuses on the shape and form of the message that SL tries to convey.

To put it another way, it is the replication of grammatical units, as well as the maintenance of coherence in word use and meanings in relation to the context of the source. The goal of the terms "Dynamic Equivalence" and "Functional Equivalence" is to get an expression that is completely natural. The theory put forward by Eugene Nida is primarily concerned with two aspects: form and impact. He said that it is impossible to produce a translation that incorporates both of these aspects.

3.4.4. Bassnett's Theory of Translation

Susan Bassnett emphasises the need for cultural awareness, or an understanding of the function culture plays in the translation process. In 1990, Susan Bassnett moved the translating model outside the realm of language studies. They compared SLT and TLT in order to investigate how culture influences translation, and they published their findings. The author of the book titled *Translation, History and Culture* takes into consideration the impact that the publishing business has had on various ideologies. There is also an examination of translation in the perspective of colonialism, as well as a discussion of feminist writing. In the chapter, "Translating Prose", of the book *Translation Studies*, the author makes the claim that because the novel seems to have a more straightforward structure than poetry does, it is accordingly easier to translate. She has witnessed the approach that pupils use when translating writing into their own words. She says that people just open the SL text and start reading from the beginning, without thinking about how the first part links to the overall organisation of the book as a whole. When it comes to her, form and substance are inextricably linked. In the same way, the translator has to have done extensive research and careful reading of the source material in SL beforehand. As evidence for her claim, she has provided an example in the form of an excerpt, which is the beginning of *The Magic Mountain*, translated by H. T. Lowe-Porter. She has also discussed the issues in this translation compared to the original German text, as well as the degree to which the SL and TL versions diverge from one another. In their book *Post-colonial Translation: Theory and Practice* (1959), Sussan Bemett and Harish Trivedi refer to translation as an uneven fight between a variety of lesser languages and the English language.

3.4.5. Venuti's Theory of Translation

He strongly emphasizes the need to expand the limits of translation styles and consider cultural concerns as a significant component of the translation process. The book *Towards a Philosophy of a Variation* is concerned with philosophical concepts. Both domestication and foreignization, often known as the connection between SL and TL in terms of culture, are discussed here. As said by Lawrence Venuti, "each translator might also view the process of translating via the prism of cultural context", which deflects the social practices of the original language. It is the task of the translator to convey these cultural norms, preserving both their meaning and their foreignness, into the text of the target language. Every stage of the translation process, from the identification of target texts to the execution of translation methodologies to the editing, reviewing, and reading of translations, is mediated by the many cultural values prevalent in the language being translated into.

In his work titled *Contemporary Translation Theories*, Edwin Gentzler provides an analysis of Lawrence Venuti's perspectives on translation. He brought attention to significant facets of Venuti's writings, which include theories of Translation. The theories of Venuti include a few original concepts; according to him, competent translators are evaluated based on how "fluently" they can read. The integrity of the text that has been translated should be such that it does not give the impression that it has been translated at all. It is intended that translations will seem to be the original work. In his opinion, there are really two distinct issues at play here. The first issue that he brings up is the marginalisation of the translator. It places the translation in a position of subservience to the author and characterises the translator's activity as being derivative and secondary. It ranks translation far lower on the priority list than creative writing. Second, it eliminates the cultural and language peculiarities of the foreign text, which the very process of translation was meant to pass over into the culture of the culture that is receiving the translation. Venuti was the first person to articulate the ethical dilemma that translators face as a binary between the processes of domestication and foreignization. The text is brought into closer conformity with the grammar of the languages as part of the domestication process. It paves the way for the acquisition of information. The process of keeping information from an SL document is referred to as foreignization, and it involves intentionally breaking the rules of the target language in order to maintain meaning. Foreignization, on the other hand, refers to the characteristic of belonging to the Source language text, while domestication refers to the process of turning the Source language message domesticated to the TL text. His research into both the philosophy and practise of translating the English language led him to the conclusion that submission and domestication predominate in the field. He is critical of translators who, for the sake of "domestication", place more weight on linguistic accuracy than cultural significance while working with SL texts. Because Venuti is a supporter of the foreignization technique, he believes that an appropriate translation is one that draws attention to the foreignness of the original text and illustrates the contrasts.

3.5. Theories of Translation from a Locational Perspective

There are various theories of translation that are predicated on the activities that took place at certain locations in history. Three main locations are examined in this text, including Chinese translation theory, Asian translation theory and the Western theory of translation. These theories of translation are further discussed in the following sections.

3.5.1. Chinese Translation Theory

During the Zhou Dynasty, interactions with vassal kingdoms were the impetus for the development of Chinese translation theory. It originated from the process of translating Buddhist text into Chinese language. This is a reaction to the abstractions of the phenomenon of translation as well as to the details of the experiences of translation from various original language into Chinese. In addition to this, it evolved within the framework of the literary and intellectual heritage of China. The individuals who resided in those five places spoke languages that could not be understood by one another, and their preferences and goals in life were distinct from one another. To make what was going on in their heads understood by others, and to convey their preferences and inclinations, there were officers who were known as transmitters in the east, representationists in the south, Ti-tis in the west, and translators in the north. These officers were strategically placed throughout the kingdom (see "The Royal Regulations", translated by James Legge and published in 1885, volume 27, pp. 229-230).

Different researchers credit Confucius with having spoken in a conversation regarding translation. Confucius gives the monarch interested in learning other languages the advice to not worry about it. Confucius advises the ruler to put their attention only on governing and to leave translation to the translators. It's possible that the saying "names may accompany their carriers, as realities would reflect China" is the first example of translation theory. Names ought to be "transliterated", but objects need to have their meanings conveyed in the translation.

Reformers such as Liang Qichao, Hu Shi, and Zhou Zuoren started studying the translation practise and philosophy of the great translators of Chinese heritage during the late Qing Dynasty and the Republican Era.

3.5.2. Asian Translation Theory

South Asia and East Asia (mainly contemporary India and China) have their translation heritage closely tied to the translation of religious literature (especially Buddhist scriptures) and the administration of the Chinese empire. Chinese translation theory outlines a number of requirements and constraints in translation, whereas ancient Indian translations are characterised by a freer adaptation than is typical in Europe.

Equally essential than translating itself in the East Asian Sinosphere (area under the cultural sway of China) has been the usage and readings of Chinese literature, which has had a significant impact on the Japanese, Korean, and Vietnamese languages via terminology and writing system borrowings. Noteworthy is Japanese Kanbun, which is a way of glossing Chinese literature for Japanese speakers.

3.5.3. Western Theory of Translation

Discussions of translation philosophy and practise may be traced back to antiquity. The ancient Greeks differentiated between metaphrase (exact translation) and paraphrase. This difference was embraced by English poet and translator John Dryden (1631-1700), who characterised translation as the intelligent mixing of these two types of phrasing when choosing, in the target language, "counterparts", or equivalents, for the terms employed in the source language.

When words have a beautiful, literal meaning, it would be a disservice to the creator to alter them. It would be unfair to force a translation to stick strictly to the words of his author; it suffices if he chooses a phrase that does not distort the meaning.

This fundamental articulation of the essential notion of translation – equivalence – is as sufficient as any that has been suggested: "since Cicero and Horace, who, in 1st-century-BCE Rome, memorably and literally" advised avoiding "word for word" translation (verbum pro verbo).

Even if there have been some theoretical shifts in this field, the practical practice of translation has altered very little since antiquity.

In summary, translators demonstrated prudence in pursuing replacements – "textual" where feasible, paraphrastic where required – for the intended sense and other essential "principles" (such as style, verse form, correlation with musical accompaniment, or, in films, with speech articulation progression), with the exception of some extraordinary contextual in the slightly earlier Christian era and the Middle Ages and "adapters in various periods".

Works Cited

Baker, M. (2004) Translation and Conflict: A Narrative Account. Abingdon: Routledge.

Boase-Beier, J. (2010) "Who needs theory?", in Translation: Theory and Practice in Dialogue, Fawcett, A., Guadarrama García, K. and Hyde Parker, R. (eds.) London and New York: Continuum. pp. 25–38.

Kim, M., Munday, J., Wang, Z., and Wang, P. (2021) Systemic Functional Linguistics and Translation Studies. London and New York: Bloomsbury.

Levý, J. (2011) The Art of Translation, trans. by P. Corness, Jettmarová, Z. (ed.) Amsterdam: John Benjamins.

Marais, K. (2018) A Semiotic Theory of Translation: The Emergence of Socio-cultural Reality. Abingdon: Routledge.

Munday, J. (2008) Companion to Translation Studies. Abingdon and New York: Routledge.

Munday, J. (2012). *Evaluation in translation: Critical points of translator decision-making*. Routledge.

Munday, J., and Zhang, M. (2015) "Discourse Analysis in Translation Studies", Special issue of Target, 27(3) pp.325–334.

Nida, E. A. (1969). Science of translation. *Language*, 483-498.

Nida, E., and Taber, C. R. (1969) The Theory and Practice of Translation. Leiden: E. J. Brill.

Robinson, D. (1997) Western Translation Theory: From Herodotus to Nietzsche. Manchester: St Jerome.

Venuti, L. (Ed.). (2021) *The translation studies reader*. Routledge.

CHAPTER FOUR

TRANSLATION TECHNIQUES AND STRATEGIES

4.1. Introducing the Concept of Translation Strategies

The translation approach or procedure that should be used has been the subject of interpretations provided by a number of research. Krings (1986) summarises translation strategy as the translator's possibly intentional approaches to resolving specific translation issues within the context of a particular translation assignment. In a similar vein, Loescher (1991) views translation strategy as a method, which may or may not be conscious, for finding a solution to a problem that arises while translating a text or any portion of it. According to what is said in this interpretation, the concept of awareness is important when differentiating the tactics utilized by those learning a language or translating it. In this respect, Cohen (1998) says that what differentiates techniques from these procedures which aren't purposeful is the presence of an element of awareness, and that this feature is what makes strategies unique. According to Lawrence Venuti (1998), translation strategies include the fundamental duties of selecting the foreign content to be translated and establishing a way to translate it. When referring to different translation processes, he makes use of the ideas of "domesticating" and "foreignizing". In addition, Venuti views strategy as a collection of skills, which may be seen as a sequence of actions or procedures that facilitate the accumulation, retrieval, and use of knowledge. He believes that strategies are of a heuristic and flexible character and that adopting a strategy entails making a choice that is impacted by changes in the translator's goals.

The method in which various academics characterise translation tactics seems to imply that the strategies are the result of a variety of different kinds of intentional attempts. As a consequence of this, the formulation of certain techniques is dependent on the work that particular translation theory scholars have accomplished.

In most cases, the translation strategies presented in published works are based on the work of a select group of researchers, as shown by an analysis of a variety of studies on translation. The translation procedures that were suggested by Vinay and Darbelnet (1973), Venuti (1995), Desline (1993), Malone (1988), and Newmark (1988) are presented in this textbook, and both explain their findings with examples drawn from a variety of languages. In order to conduct an in-depth analysis of the nature of the translation techniques suggested by each of the researchers, each of the scholars has been designated a section in this chapter.

4.2. Translation Strategies According to Vinay and Darbelnet (1973)

In the 1950s, two French researchers by the names of Jean-Paul Vinay and Jean Darbelnet conducted research on the linguistic characteristics of translation. Since Translation Studies was not a particularly well-developed topic at the time, much of the research Vinay and Darbelnet conducted was categorised under the umbrella of Comparative Literature. When looking at the work that Vinay and Darbelnet have done, the word contrastive linguistics appears to be a lot better fit since what they did was compare and contrast two or more languages in order to improve their knowledge of both of them. Vinay and Darbelnet's research concentrated on the procedure of translation, in contrast to that of other researchers who just attempted to contrast two languages in an attempt to get insight into the connection that exists between them. Their efforts culminated in what is considered to be their collection of essays in the linguistic switch of translation studies. The title of this work is *Stylistique comparée du Français et de L'anglais: Méthode de Traduction*, and approximately 40 years later it was translated into an English version and given the title *Comparative Stylistics of French and English: A Methodology for Translation*. The realisation that it continued to be considered essential enough to translate into English over half a century after its first publication demonstrates just how significant it was. According to the theory that Vinay and Darbelnet presented in their book, there are seven primary processes or procedures that are in play whenever a translation is carried out. These are the seven suggestions that the researchers developed.

4.2.1. Borrowing Strategy

In a nutshell, the act of taking a phrase or expression from one language and using it in another language, but doing so in a manner that is more natural to that language, is what is meant by the term "borrowing". When it is required for a more accurate manner of translation, one should utilise it (Vinay & Darbelnet, 2000; Munday 2001). The process of taking words straight from one language and using them in another without first translating them is known as borrowing. Many terms derived from the English language have been "borrowed" and used in other languages, such as "software" in the area of technology and "funk" in the field of culture. Additionally, various terms from other languages have been adopted into English. These words include abattoir, café, passé, and résumé from the French language; hamburger and kindergarten from the German language; and bandana, musk, and sugar from the Sanskrit language. When borrowed words are regarded to be "foreign," they are often written with the italics font style. If a translator is not one of those individuals who get lending and borrowing mixed up, then this should not be too challenging. The concept of borrowing refers to taking a term from the language that serves as the source (SL) and incorporating it into the language that serves as the target (TL). It is considered to be the simplest of the procedures, and it is typically used in one of two scenarios: "either when discussing a fresh, complex mechanism in which no concept remains within the Source language, or when preserving a word from the source language (SL) for aesthetic impacts, that requires the translator deploying the foreign concept to add flavour to the target text" (Munday, 2001, p.9).

Typically, it is employed in the context of new specialized or undiscovered notions in order to get around a metalinguistic problem. In all other aspects, borrowing is a technique of translation in which the form of the source language is adopted into the target language, and this is often done because there is a gap in the lexical resources available in the target language. The process of borrowing is the most straightforward of all the steps involved in translating. Borrowing is used for a variety of purposes, the most common of which is to express a taste characteristic of the source language. However, borrowing may also be utilised to convey a sound impact and to guarantee that a cultural component is not translated out of existence. Take, for instance, the verb "mailer", which appears in Canadian-French utterances. To make the English verb "mail" correspond to the requirements of French verb formation, the French suffix "er" is added to the end of the verb (Harding & Riley, 1986).

Also, the Swahili language accumulates words from other languages the globalised languages. For example, the terms "droni", "kombora la kibalisti", and "mzinga wa roketi", which are derived from the English terms "drone", "ballistic missile", and "rocket launcher", respectively; and the terms "zaka", "rahimu", "sukran", and "hadith", which are derived from Arabic terms.

4.2.2. Transposition Strategy

When words are translated into another language, this is the technique through which the order in which certain elements of speech are spoken is altered, for instance "blue ball" in English can be translated as "boule bleue" in French). One may say that there has been a change in the category of the term. The structures of various languages' grammatical systems are often distinct from one another. The expression in English "he enjoys swimming" can be translated to be "Er schwimmt gern" in the German language. Since the Spanish prefers to place the verb in a different spot in the phrase than the English does, transposition is a common practise when translating between the two languages. In English, the verb will typically appear somewhere close to the beginning of the phrase, but in Spanish, it may appear anywhere closer to the conclusion. This requires the translator to be aware that it is relatively easy to substitute a text classification in the TL "without modifying the meaning of the source text" (Munday, 2001). For instance, the English phrase "hand knitted" (noun + participle) becomes the Spanish phrase "tejido a mano" (participle + adverbial phrase). Vinay and Darbelnet described the procedure of transposition as switching word classes without altering the meaning. This term refers to the process through which translators alter the word type, often without giving it much thought. An example of this would be changing nouns into verbs. Vinay and Darbelnet thought that transposition was either necessary or unnecessary, and they alluded to the ST as the representation of the foundation and indeed the TT as the representation of the transposition.

In summary, transposition is a method that includes swapping the word class of one word with that of another word without altering the meaning of the message. It discusses differences in grammatical structure brought by translation (Vinay & Darbelnet, 2000; Fawcett, 1997). There are two distinct kinds of transposition, namely mandatory transposition and voluntary transposition. The term "obligatory transposition" refers to situations in which the target language does not have any other options because the language system requires the translator to make some syntactical modifications to make the translated text intelligible and grammatically acceptable by the readers of the target language. However, the translator has the freedom to choose whether or not to use optional transposition, and they are able to do so whenever they deem it essential for achieving a more accurate manner of translations (Vinay & Darbelnet; 2000, Munday 2001).

Transposition, in its most basic form, refers to the process by which the order in which portions of speech are presented in a translated text might alter. As mentioned by Zakhir (2010), this method is often used by translators due to the fact that it provides them with a number of choices that assist in avoiding issues relating to the inability to be translated.

4.2.3. Calque Strategy

When a translator replicates the structure or way of expression of the source text (ST) in their own translation, a calque, also known as Through-Translation as described by Newmark (1988), is produced. It's possible that calque will add a structure that's not present in the TL. In the exact words of Catherine (2012), native speakers of Swahili are accustomed to using the expressions "hatua ya mtoano", "kombe la dunia", "kupanga matokeo", "kutetea ubingwa", and "mabingwa wa ulaya", which are an imitation of the English expressions "knockout stage", "world cup", "to fix a match", and "to defend championship".

A calque is a specific kind of borrowing that occurs when the translator takes a term directly from the text being borrowed from and then literally translates every portion of the original contents. It may be in the lexical system or it could be in the foundation components of the TL text. There are instances when calques are successful and other times when they are not.

A phrase that is taken from one language and literally translated into another is known as a calque. The term "calque" is a calque of "loan translation", which is a calque of the German word "Lehnübersetzung". One will often find them in specialised or internationalised industries like "quality assurances" (aseguramiento de calidad, assurance qualité adopted from English). Examples of words that have been assimilated into the English language include "standpoint" and beer garden, which were borrowed from the German Standpunkt as well as Biergarten, and breakfast, which was borrowed from the French word "déjeuner" (which is now implies lunch in Europe but still means breakfast in Québec).

For the vast majority of people, the meaning of other calques may be fairly cryptic, particularly when they pertain to specialised professions or fields of study like law and science. The word "solución de compromiso" is a Spanish legal concept that was borrowed from the English phrase "compromise solution". Although Spanish lawyers are familiar with the term, the meaning is not immediately understood by the average Spanish citizen. A failed calque may be exceedingly unnatural, and it can produce unintentional comedy, which is sometimes misunderstood as an indication that the translator does not have sufficient skill in the chosen language. A calque occurs when a phrase taken from the source text (ST) is translated word for word into the target text (TT). Calques may either translate each word literally while adhering to the syntax of the TL, or they can disregard the grammar of the TL and adhere to the grammar of the SL, which results in the calque having an unusual syntactical structure when it is rendered in the TT.

4.2.4. Trans-Literation (Literal Translation)

Depending on the form of the original comment, a word-for-word translation may be appropriate in certain languages while it is not appropriate in others. The phrase "El equipo está trabajando para terminar el informe" would be translated into English as "The team is working hard to finish the report". It is successful most of the time, but there are also occasions when it is not. The grammatical structures in the source language are transformed to their closest counterparts in the target language, while the lexical terms often are translated separately and devoid of context. This is an indication of the issues that need to be resolved as part of the process of re-translation.

The above statement in Spanish, for instance, cannot be translated into either French or German employing this method due to the fact that the sentence patterns in French and German are quite different from one another. It is not the case that every statement can be literally translated into another language just because one sentence may be literally translated into another language. "El equipo experimentado está trabajando para terminar el informe" translates into English as "The knowledgeable staff are hard at work trying to complete the reports" ("experienced" and "team" are reversed). As stated by Vinay and Darbelnet, this typical method of translation is not to be used outside of certain parameters unless absolutely necessary. The two researchers agree that an appropriate application of literal translation is the concept of translating a text word for word in a manner that does not affect the sense of the original text. To put it more simply, literal translation broadens the application of a calque in a manner that is far more socially acceptable.

Vinay and Darbelnet (Munday, 2001) characterise literal translation as one of the much prevalent translation technique utilised among two languages that belong to the same family and heritage. Literal translation involves the direct transfer of the source text into a target text that is grammatical and idiomatically appropriate. When using this method, the translator places a significant amount of emphasis on ensuring that the translation adheres closely to the linguistic conventions of the source language.

When it comes to literal translation, this refers to the process of replacing syntactic structures of the source language, which are typically on the clause or sentence scale, with syntactic structures of the target language that are isomorphic to the source structures and are synonymous with regard to the content they convey. The direct translation of the English phrase "where are you?" in French is "où êtes-vous?" As said by Vinay and Darbelnet, literal translation is often prevalent when transferring between two languages that are members of the same language family and much more so when translating between languages that are part of the same culture. There is considerable convergence in structure and concept across the European languages, and because of this "literal translations between English and French" are sometimes acceptable. It is important to point out that, in their view, there is no conceptual difference between literal translation and translation, that is, a word for word equivalent.

4.2.5. Modulation Strategy

Modulation may be considered as "a shift in the points of view or a modification of viewpoint while transforming the information from the ST into the TT", as stated by Vinay and Darbelnet (1958/1995, pp.249-255) and Newmark (1988, p.88), respectively. According to Vinay and Darbelnet (1958/1995, p.37), modulation may either be mandatory or fixed, optional or free, or it can be free entirely. They believe that constant modulation is used by taking into consideration "the frequency of usage, the general approval, and the confirmation offered by a vocabulary or grammar of the desired term". Free modulations are "single examples, not yet set and sanctioned by use", and they provide a one-of-a-kind solution that is obligatory rather than voluntary. They clarify that a free modulation may become permanent if it is employed frequently enough, when it gives the sole answer, when it is referenced in dictionaries and grammars, and when it is consistently taught. Modulation is the process of modifying the language that is achieved by shifting one's point of view; this shift may be rationalised, even if it is taken literally or transposed. The majority of the time, it is used to emphasise the message, to effect coherence, or to discover natural shape in the TL.

The process of modulation involves communicating the same thought utilising sentence that is unique to the language being modulated into rather than the language being modulated from. "Te lo dejo" translates literally as "I leave it to you", however, the phrase "You can have it" is more accurate. The semantics are altered, and the viewpoint of the original text is shifted as a result. Without changing the message's content and without causing the audience of the target language feel uneasy, the translator may create a new point of view for the recipient of the message by using a technique called modulation. It is used rather often within a single language. Examples of modulation include the phrases "es fácil de entender" (which literally translates to "it is simple to comprehend") and "no es complicado de entender" (which literally translates to "it is not tough to grasp"). It is not challenging to comprehend indicates a prior assumption of difficulty, which we are refusing to acknowledge by insisting that it is not difficult to comprehend whereas it is effortless to comprehend simply communicates "easiness". Although both phrases communicate identical interpretation, it is straightforward to comprehend simply conveys "easiness". This particular shift in perspective, which occurs inside a message, is what causes a reader to agree and say, "Yes, this is precisely how we express it in our language". Modulation is the sixth process that Vinay and Darbelnet have developed. The term "modulation" describes the process of depicting the TT from a point of view that is distinct from the ST. Vinay and Darbelnet believe that it is required to carry out this method if the outcomes of the other procedures would result in a translation that sounded odd while being accurate grammatically, syntactically, and lexically. The translator may achieve a measure of interpretability in their TT by the use of modulation, which allows them to do so without compromising the meaning or correctness of the source text (ST). A fantastic example that Vinay and Darbelnet presented demonstrates how the double negative construction often used in English is unusual in French and how modulation would convert this in French as a simple affirmative remark employing a positive modifier.

In a nutshell, modulation refers to a change in the shape of the message that comes about as a consequence of a shift in perspective. It suggests a shift in the vantage point from something that is seen. Vinay and Darbelnet differentiate between mandatory and optional modulation when it comes to translation strategies. This form of translation method is used when, despite the fact that the translated content is grammatically accurate, it is judged inappropriate in the TL. The phrase "the time when" is an excellent illustration of compulsory modulation since it must be translated as "le moment où", which in back-translation means "the moment when", and not literally as "the moment where". The form of modulation that includes changing a negative SL word into an optimistic TL statement is referred to as optional modulation. One example of this type of modulation is the phrase "it is not easy", which may be translated as "it is difficult". Sometimes a voluntary modulation will relate to the circumstance described in the SL text so precisely that it will be required to use it.

4.2.6. Adaptation and Equivalence

Apart from the aforementioned and discussed strategies, Vinay and Darbelnet also proposed adaptation and equivalence as functional translation methods. When a scenario from the source text did not actually apply in the culture of the target language, adaptation is the process of adjusting the cultural reference to reflect the new circumstances. Vinay and Darbelnet (1958, p.91) give an example of an Englishman who, without paying much attention, "kisses his daughter on the lips" as a welcome of a wonderful parent after a long travel. Vinay and Darbelnet use this Englishman as an example to illustrate their point. However, if you were to literally translate the phrase "He kissed his daughter on the lips", it would definitely seem strange to an audience in French since the phrase may have a different meaning in that country. As a consequence of this, translating anything into French calls for a very particular form of over-rendering.

Taking into consideration the aforementioned procedures, Mashhady, Pourgalavi, and Fatollahi (2015, p.59) asserted that the preliminary different strategies primarily deal with the language elements of translations and the conceptual differences between two languages. In contrast, the last three procedures primarily concentrate on conveying the contextual components of language. When something that is unique to one language culture is presented in a completely different form that is familiar or suitable to another language culture, this is an example of adaptation. There has been a change in the cultural atmosphere. Should the meal known as pincho, which is often seen on the menu of Spanish restaurants, be translated into English as kebab? Shifting the cultural element when a circumstance from the source texts may not apply in the culture of the target language is an example of what is involved in this process.

On the other hand, equivalency refers to the process of exchanging a situation from one language for a communicatively analogous one in another language. The vast majority of equivalences are set, and they are employed in the translation process for idiom, parables, verbal or attributive phrases, and other similar expressions. In general, equivalences are best shown via the use of proverbs. Therefore, "it is raining cats and dogs" is the literal translation of the French phrase "il pleut a seaux/des cordes".

According to Vinay and Darbelnet (1995, p.342), translation is a process that re-creates the same scenario as the original text while using language that is entirely distinct from that of the source text. They also indicate that if this approach is performed throughout the process of translation, it may keep the stylistic effect of the source language text in the target language. This is something that they have found to be the case. According to them, equivalency is thus the best strategy to use when the translator is tasked with dealing with idioms, metaphors, cliches, nominal or adjectival phrases, and the onomatopoeia of animal noises. This is because these types of phrases are notoriously difficult to translate.

To summarise, equivalency is often advantageous for the translator to use a completely different arrangement with a variety of meanings from that of the text written in the source language so long as it is deemed acceptable in the discourse community that is equivalent to that of the text written in the source language. This is the case so long as the translator is translating the text from one language into another.

4.2.7. Summarizing Vinay and Darbelnet's Translation Strategies

The categorization of translation methods into required and voluntary categories is an essential component of the method used by Vinay and Darbelnet. On either the grammatical or vocabulary level, one will find the methods necessary for obligatory translation. They fall under the "category of non-literal translation techniques" because they are driven by variations in the structural, semantic, or sociocultural components of the source and target languages. "Obligatory changes in syntax", which Vinay and Darbelnet discuss under the title "servitude", take place when the translator, in his attempt to portray an ST, is obliged to discover new methods of expressing it in the TL. Vinay and Darbelnet refer to these kinds of modifications as "obligatory changes in syntax". In addition to this, compulsory lexical rearrangement is required if a particular idea from the SL texts is lacking in the TL text. Optional shifts, on the other hand, are attributed to the style and preferences of the translator, in contrast to the mandatory translation methods. In situations like these, the decisions that the translator makes may rely on a variety of things, including the sort of content that is to be translated, the audience that is intended for the translation, and the translator's preferences about style. However, in many instances, the distinction between translation procedures that are optional and those that are required seems to be rather subjective, and it may be difficult to determine which of the two options is more appropriate.

Their theory has been an extensive effort to arrange a variety of occurrences into a number of categories and subcategories of translation processes, and as a result, it has produced strategies of translating that can be used to the text that will serve as the target. However, there has been a lot of backlash directed at the classification approach that they use. It is possible that the incorporation of borrowing into the categorization system would be deemed inappropriate due to the fact that a direct borrowing cannot be regarded a translation method in the stricter meaning of the term (Wills, 1982, p.100). Both calque and literal translation, on the other hand, cannot be seen to be straightforward translation processes but rather two distinct applications of translation. The four techniques for oblique translation are all impacted when there is confusion over the limits of categories. Therefore, the usage of the word "equivalence" to denote the sixth translation method is problematic given that the goal of each and every translation process is to achieve equivalence, which may be achieved by selecting any translation processes. In a similar vein, the concept of "adaptation" contains a broad range of connotations, any one of which might accurately describe the process of non-literal translation.

4.3. Peter Newmark's Translation Strategies

The translation framework proposed by Newmark takes into account both the text and the function of the language. According to Newmark, translation is simply the act of converting one language into another. In the research conducted by Jacobson and Buler, the three primary roles of language were identified as the expressive function, the information function, and the vocative function. He came to the conclusion that the vast majority of texts complete these three duties in some capacity. In order for translators to be successful in translating the same material and even the same section, they need use a variety of translation processes and methodologies. The technique of translation must be determined based on the primary purpose of the material. That is to suggest, for the particular text, the primary purpose determines the job that the translator is engaged in, which includes style, unit, language kinds, inadequate meaning, neologisms, critical words, and metaphors, etc. Newmark lays the groundwork for the reference to the translator, who should use various translation approaches in order to work toward the goal of producing on its readers an impact that is as similar as possible to the effect that was acquired on the users of the source material. As a result, Newmark supports the idea of using multiple translation procedures according to the kind of content being translated. Newmark is the author of a number of influential translation ideas, and he is also responsible for categorising the many kinds of translated texts.

Newmark is the author of a number of influential translation ideas, and he is also responsible for categorising the many kinds of translated texts. In his book, *Translation Problem Explore*, the primary focus is on his proposed technique of translation, which he refers to as semantic and communicative translation. According to Newmark, the goal of communicative translation is to achieve on the part of its readers an impact that is as comparable as feasible to what was accomplished on the part of readers of the original text. The goal of semantic translation is to convey the precise interpretation of the source text (taking into account contextual factors) in the target language in a manner that is semantically and syntactically accurate to the greatest extent possible. Theoretically, the two approaches diverge rather significantly from one another (Newmark, 1988, p.39).

Numerous strategies of translation were suggested by various scholars as a means of researching and analysing the linguistic shifts that occur as a result of the act of translation. These models have been developed in an effort to investigate and investigate the linguistic shifts that occur.

In effort to investigate and investigate the linguistic shifts that occur. Due to the fact that Newmark's model of translation operations is an all-encompassing model, it was chosen to be used in this research. Newmark (1988) presents a total of 16 methods of translation, which include "synonymy," "through-translation," "shift or transposition," "modulation," recognised "translation", "compensation", "componential analysis," "reduction and expansion", "paraphrase", couplets, and notes. Other methods include transference, naturalisation, "cultural equivalent", "functional equivalent", and descriptive equivalent. All the translation strategies proposed by Newmark are presented below numerically.

1. Transference: As defined by Newmark (1988, p.8), transference is "the method of converting a Source language text to a Translated text". For instance, "Jihad" is what the term "جههاد" means when translated into English. Whenever there is no comparable method in TL, this technique is utilised instead.

2. Naturalization: According to Newmark (1988), naturalisation is the process of a phrase from one language being adapted to the pronunciation and word forms of another language. For example, the term "philosophy " is translated to Arabic as "فلسفة".

3. Cultural Equivalent: According to Newmark (1988), the cultural equivalent technique is a close translation of a cultural phrase from a different language into the language of the target culture. For example, "best regards" is translated into Arabic as " وواالسلامم علـيیكم ووررحمة لله ووبركاتـهه" which is considered to be the cultural equivalent (Tanjour, 2011, p.52). Due to the fact that it does not provide reliable results, the culture equivalent technique is only useful to a limited extent.

4. Functional Equivalent: As described by Newmark (1988), the functional equivalent approach "needs the employment of a culture-free word, sometimes in conjunction with a new particular term" (p. 83). As an example, the term "dress" is rendered into its operational equivalent in Arabic as "ثوب" (Tanjour, 2011, p.134).

5. Descriptive Equivalent: As said by Newark (1988), the term "descriptive equivalent" refers to the process of providing the TL with an explanation of the ST statement using multiple words. Different from the "functional equivalent", the "descriptive equivalent" focuses on characterising the cultural manifestation. The "descriptive equivalent" and "functional equivalent" are crucial factors in translation. For instance, the term "طشت" is translated into its English counterpart using the phrase "aluminium basin".

6. Synonymy: Newmark (1988) uses the term "synonymy" to relate to an approximated TL equivalent of a Source language term whenever there is no accurate counterpart in the TL. This is the case when there is no exact equivalent in the TL. According to Newmark (1988), this method is used where there is no obvious counterpart and the word in question does not play a substantial role in the content of the passage. For instance, the Arabic term "فساتين ززااههههيية" may be translated into English as "gorgeous outfits".

7. Loan Translation: As said by Newmark (1988), the literal translation of popular collocations, names of organisations, and the components of compounds may be accomplished by translation or through the use of loan translation (p.84). For instance, the English phrase "secondary school" may be rendered into Arabic as "المدررسة الثانوية".

8. Reorganizations or Repositioning: Translation shifts, as defined by Newmark (1988), are grammatical modifications that occur while moving from the SL into the TL. He divides them up into four distinct categories. The first form of grammatical shift is one that occurs because of grammatical discrepancies between the source text (ST) and the target text (TT). For example, the solitary word "information" in English is translated into the plural form "معلوماتت" in Arabic. The second sort of shift involves altering the sentence construction of the SL due to the fact that the TL does not include the grammatical construction used in the SL. When the literal translation of the ST is grammatically permissible, but its feel is difficult in the TL, the third form of shift is utilised. The replacement of a grammatical structure in the ST with a linguistic component in the TL is the fourth kind of shift that might occur.

9. Modulations: As shown by Newmark (1988), modulation is when a message from the ST is reworded or altered in the TL text due to differences in opinions between the SL and TL. For instance, the English word "she lived with her stepmother" can be rendered into a noun comparable in meaning as in the phrase " عاشت مع ززووجة الابـيـيـهها".

10. Translation That Is Recognized: As said by Newmark (1988), the use of an approved translation of an institutionalized term is the practise of acknowledged translation. To provide one example, the word "national bank" is rendered in Arabic as "البنك الأهلي".

11. Compensation: According to Newmark (1988), compensation takes place "when loss of meaning, sound effect, metaphor, or pragmatic impact in one portion of a phrase is compensated in another section, or in a contiguous sentence". Compensation may even take place inside the same sentence (p.90). For example, the formal Arabic line "سعدنا بلقائكم" is "translated into English" as "We are glad to see you, sir". The Arabic statement has been given a more respectful tone by the addition of the word "sir" in this particular example.

12. Reduction and expansion: In a lot of situations, compression and expansions are carried out in an instinctive manner. Due to the absence of an exact counterpart in the TL, expansion involves re-expressing the meaning of an SL term via the use of additional words in the target translation (TT). On the contrary, reduction entails leaving out parts of the ST that are deemed to be irrelevant.

13. Paraphrase: Following Newmark (1988), the purpose of using paraphrase is to show the interpretation of a portion of a text; this is especially useful when there are substantial implications. The English expression "All this was water on the Master's mill" is translated into Arabic as " كان هذا كله مفيدا لخطة الأمم".

14. Couplets: According to Newmark (1988), the couplets translation technique takes place when a translator employs the use of two distinct methods in order to address a single issue. For instance, "Google" is rendered to Arabic as "متصفح قوقل". This is only one example. This particular example makes use of not one, but two different procedures: the transcribing technique, and the paraphrase procedure.

15. Notes: Writing notes process, as described by Newmark (1988), involves "supplying more information in a translation". It's possible that a translator may need to use this method in order to supplement the text with additional information that's cultural, linguistic, or technical. There are three different places where notes may be added:

inside the body of the text itself, at the end of a pages, or at the conclusion of a chapter or book.

4.4. Malone's Translation Strategies

Malone lists nine techniques that translators can adopt at the morphological as well as lexicogrammatical dimension: equations, substitutions, divergent, convergent, amplifying, reducing, diffusing, condensing, and rearranging. The very first eight are typically given as pairs because they are symmetrical and mutually reinforcing to each other as well. The different translation strategies as proposed by Malone are discussed below.

1. **Equation**: The most straightforward interpretation of Equation is that of the borrowing term, in which case equality would appear to be an absolute. For example, the "Italians play football and the English eat lasagna". In spite of the fact that the translation of rucola into rocket would be provided by a bilingual dictionary, rucola is currently widely available in English grocery stores. Italians enjoy "un po' di relax as frequently as un riposo". It is necessary to call into question the absolute equivalency of these terms given that they are utilised on text in contexts other than those in which they are often used. Even if lasagna is now a common part of the diet in the United Kingdom, the term "lasagna" will not evoke the same associations in the minds of British people as it does among Italians. The calque is a second version of equation that is provided by the target language adapting the term of the source language to fit within the language's morpho-phonological structure. This form of equation is known as the calque. The Italian football phrases "dribblare" and "crossare", which originated from the English verbs "to dribble" and "to cross", respectively, are now deeply ingrained in the language. Given that English lacks gender and plural markers for adjectives, another illustration of this is the exclamation of approval known as "Bravo", which is spoken in the English language and is typically used in musical contexts. Bravo can be directed to one or multiple individuals of either gender.

2. **Substitution**: To return to Malone's language, the opposite of Equation is Substitution, which is used in situations where there is hardly any straightforward equivalency. Substitution can be thought of as the "antithesis" of Equation. For instance, on a level that is strictly related to grammar, the prepositional phrase in Italian

"replaces substitutes" "the English Saxon genitive": Gulliver's Travels = I "Viaggidi Gulliver". An English infinitive may be used for the Italian subjunctive in the following sentences: " Farò in modo che si interessi", "I will make an effort to convince her to".

The idiom "The straw that broke the camel's back" has been superseded by the Italian expression "La goccia che fa traboccare il vaso", which refers to a smaller object that causes a larger object to topple over. In the 1951 adaptation of "Alice in Wonderland" produced by Walt Disney Pictures, Alice was assigned a song to perform at the commencement of the movie. The song is titled "Cats and Rabbits", and it is all about cats and rabbits. Those who put in the effort to translate will ensure that their substitutions include compensatory measures. "There'd Be New Birds" is the third verse of the song, and it goes as follows:

"Gli uccellini are always cheerful, affable, and cute. There are a great many of them, and they are called howdy do birds. Within that universe of my own, known as questo mio mondo ideal, everyone would have a dozen blue birds singing an aria by Puccini in their cages."

In the translation, many artistic liberties have been taken; for example, the quatrain has been extremely obviously "substituted." Although the causes for the change are not only linguistic (there are concerns of rhyme, of scanning, and of cultural displacement), it is clear that from the very beginning, linguistic faithfulness had to be abandoned in order to serve a greater aim, which was the pleasure of children.

3. **Divergence**: It illustrates the one-to-many link that exists between individuals. The tactic of divergence entails selecting an appropriate term from amongst a variety of possibilities for use as alternatives. It's possible that there's a restricted variety of options available, such as cream = panna or crema, or there may be a confusing selection, such as "girare" = to rotate, to turn around, to carry over, to turn, to turn around, to evade, to cruise, to journey, to advocate, to engage, to blast, to whirl, to cluster, to blow, etc. Both the meaning and the functionality of the Italian recurrence adverb "sempre" can be understood to be distinct from one another, as seen below"

   i. "Viene sempre di venerdì"
      Fridays are his day of arrival each and every week.

   ii. "Il Napoli preme ma la Juventus è sempre primo in classifica"
      Even if Napoli is ramping up their efforts, Juventus continue to maintain their lead in the table.

4. **Convergence**: It illustrates the many-to-one link that exists between the two entities. The concept of convergence is diametrically opposed to that of divergence. In one of the few examples of Italian that Malone provides, he explains how the personal pronouns tu, Lei, voi, and Loro can all be interpreted as "you," depending on the setting in which they are used. In a business setting, the three Italian phrases commercialista, ragioniere, and contabile would converge to offer the unique translation equivalence accountants in the vast majority of instances when converting to English without generating undue discomfort.

5. **Amplification**: For this reason, the translator will need to include some new material into the source text in order to make it more easily understandable. The note added by the translator, which may appear as an endnote, a footnote, or as a delimited extension preceding the item that is being discussed, is the type of amplification that is most readily apparent. Occasionally, a particular lexeme from a language necessitates a lexicogrammatical collaborator in order for it to be understood correctly in subsequent occurrences.

   Amplification is also necessary in situations whenever the SL "takes for granted" essential elements. These components could be cultural, semantic, or linguistic, or a combination of these and other factors. "Dopo la battaglia di Courtrai" is the example that Giuseppina Cortese (2000) uses to demonstrate how to translate "after Courtrai" into Italian for a piece that is not intended for history scholars. In order to facilitate the reader's understanding of complex material, technical writing frequently makes use of the amplification device.

6. **Reduction**: As its name suggests, involves leaving out components of a target text on the grounds that they are superfluous or perhaps give the reader the wrong impression. The phrase "carta geografica" in Italian translates literally to "map" in English, whereas the term "three-toed sloth" in English translates to "bradipo" in Italian. The author and translator Tim Parks (1994) provides the example of an order regarding what to do with one's parking ticket that said in Italian "Esporre in modo visibile," which can be translated as "Display". Parks presents this example to illustrate the point.

7. **Diffusion**: In order to give a certain amount of embellishment in the chosen language, a text item from the source text is stretched without introducing any alternative layers of meaning. For example: "Magari!" needs to be assimilated into a locution along the lines of "If only I could Would that it were!" That is something one really hope to be true! The use of subjunctive and conditional constructions

in Italian can convey a wide variety of meanings, which frequently necessitates the application of diffusing in English translation. The perfect conditional demands the use of a typical passive voice expression of the kind. For example, "La banda avrebbe rapinato altre trebanche" is a statement that uses the perfect conditional. It is suspected that the group has committed bank robberies at a total of three more locations. According to reports, the criminal organisation was responsible for the heist of three additional banks. It has been alleged that the gang has committed bank robberies at three additional locations.

Similarly, the ubiquitous usage of the inadequate version of the Italian verb "dovere" in situations such as "Doveva arrivare alle tre" needs to be diffused to "He was meant to come at three o'clock".

8. **Condensation**: Condensation is the process of reducing the length of a source text without removing any of the meaning's underlying layers. The expression in the target text is one that makes better use of language. It is generally accepted that the English language is more concise than the Italian language. Certain popular adverbs and verbal expressions, on the other hand, can be shortened. For example, "a buon prezzo, a buon mercato" might be shortened to "cheap far vedere" to demonstrate the same meaning. In the opposing approach, prepositional verbs as well as phrasal verbs are classic examples of this phenomena. For example, to gaze at is equivalent to the Italian word guardare, to make up is equivalent to the Italian word "inventare", and to make up for is equivalent to the Italian word compensare.

9. **Reordering**: As we move on to the tactic of Reordering, we enter the realm of comparative syntax. At its most fundamental level, this tactic requires the translator to perform fundamental inversion procedures, such as with adjective-noun sequences (such as white horse/cavallo bianco) and verb-object positioning (such as (io) ti amo/I love you). However, it is also vitally important for the translator to be aware of the circumstances in which these mechanisms should not be activated, whether for grammatical or rhetorical reasons. "Pressione alta" is the translation that should be used for "high pressure" in the context of medicine; however, "alta pressione" should be used when referring to "banks of high pressure" in the context of Italian meteorology. While the desperate admirer is attempting to wring (estorcere, strappare) the critical words "Ti amo" from his loved one, he may lay emphasis on his own feelings by saying "ma io amo te!".

4.5. General Translation Strategies

Apart from the above discussed translation strategies that are primarily predicated on different researchers, there are other translation methods. There are a plethora of translation methods that are developed consistently by different researcher order than the ones discussed already.

One general translation method is the "word by word translation". It is distinguished by the precise replication of linguistic components taken from the original text; in other words, it is a translation that is word for word. There should be no alterations made to the literary style or language. It is essential that the morphology, syntax, and/or interpretation of the source text be faithfully preserved. Because the focus here is not change but rather recreating the grammatical structure or the structuring of the original text, the functionality of the translations may be susceptible to some modification after it has been translated.

Free translation is another translation method. it is the goal of "free translation" is to maintain the functionality of the original language, even if this results in a loss of meaning for the overall message. The content cannot be altered in any way. It is acceptable to make certain adjustments to categories such as the social and cultural setting, the genre, or the communicative component (tonality, dialect). These alterations may vary depending on the target audience (for example, if the work is intended for children), the additional classification (stage modification), the change in context, or the author's personal decision. Before we can translate "freely," we need to take into consideration the categories that are prone to change, even though this technique has the advantage of being the simplest to implement. However, it cannot be used with every kind of text.

There is also the philological translation technique. When using this strategy, the translator could add comments of philological as well as contextual disposition to the translated version, not just for the reason of comprehending specific words and utterances appropriately, but also for the purposes of including explanations of recognisable interpretations; in this particular instance, the source text frequently may become the focus of evaluation, and the translation is aimed at specialised audiences or students.

Additionally, a crucial part of the whole procedure is played by what is known as the translation approach. There are many different tactics, each of which stands for a distinct technique and approach, and all of which contribute to the total translation. The translator, based on how they personally approach the process, will determine the method that will be used for the translation. There are also specialised translation strategies, which are the distinctive verbal operations, that are recognised in the final product;

these approaches accomplish transition and influence more compact units of text.

The translation process itself is quite specialised, but the approach and the tactics employed are up to the discretion of the translator and are a matter of personal taste. They are not required to be used in conjunction with one another; for instance, when employing the free translation approach, writers are free to use a variety of translation tactics and procedures. Certainly, so long as it maintains the integrity of the final product.

Works Cited

Krings, H. (1986) "Translation problems and translation strategies of advanced German learners of French (L2)", in Interlingual and Intercultural Communication: Discourse and Cognition in Translation, J. House and S. Blum-Kulka (eds.) Tübingen: Gunter Narr, pp. 262–76.

Munday, J. (2001) Introducing Translation Studies: Theories and Applications, London and New York: Routledge, 1st edition.

Newmark, P. (1988) A Textbook of Translation. New York and London: Prentice-Hall

Venuti, L. (1995) The Translator's Invisibility. A History of Translation. London: Routledge.

Venuti, L. (1998) The Translation Studies Reader, London and New York: Routledge.

Vinay, J. & P. Darbelnet. (1995) Comparative Stylistics of French and English: A Methodology for Translation, trans. And ed. J. C. Sager and M. J. Hamel, Amsterdam: Benjamins.

CHAPTER FIVE

VARIOUS CONCEPTS IN TRANSLATION STUDIES

5.1. Introduction

The study of translation, along with its many practical applications, has, over many years, resulted in the creation of several fundamental principles that support the field of translation in its broadest sense. These ideas include the notion of fidelity, fidelity erosion, transparency, equivalence, terminology, and both machine translation and technical translation. The list is not restricted to the notions that have been listed above, but these are the ones that are given importance in this chapter.

5.2. Fidelity and Fidelity Erosion in Translation

The question of fidelity in translation efforts has emerged as one of the foremost passionately disputed topics in a wide range of studies conducted by translators and theorists. Nonetheless, it remains a topic of contemporary importance. Fidelity and faithfulness in translation were in contrast to early intellectual debates. Those who subscribe to these theories believe that fidelity requires an unwavering commitment to preserving the author's voice and the integrity of the text's original context. As perfect bilingualism is unlikely to achieve, it is unclear whether or not the practise could ever be implemented. The conclusion is that it has been claimed that the idea of fidelity in translation has been shredded to an infinitesimal point.

The idea of fidelity is crucial to the field of translation since it prompts the issue of what practical use faithfulness may provide to a translator. First, one must recognise the difference "between faithfulness and what is known as literal translation", or a word-for-word rendition of the original text. According to Claudia and Brian (2016), literal translation is the process of reproducing a term or phrase in the target language exactly as it was written in the source language, without changing the meaning or adjusting for context. Fidelity, on the other hand, is the characteristic of being faithful to the original and consistent all through the text, so that the meaning and subtlety of the original text is accurately conveyed in the translated text (Claudia and Brian, 2016). As various translators are faithful to different features of the original text, translation may be seen as a subjective process. This notion of subjectivity is critical to bear in mind. Some authors are more faithful to the conventions of the language they want to write in, while others are more accurate to the culture of that language. This has led to a real debate between "dowsers", or those closest to the text's original source, and "targeters", or those closer to the text's ultimate goal, in the area of translation. The problem of quantifying loss of accuracy in translation has not yet been addressed. Although it may be difficult to quantify the extent to which translation improves upon the original language, this has not stopped investigators from focusing on just that.

The degree to which the original text and tone of a source text are maintained in a translated version of the same material remains the standard by which translators are judged on their fidelity erosion. Whether or not an accurate translation is feasible is the question that needs to be resolved. Nida (1964) made a pertinent observation on this subject, saying that each kind of communication has the risk of information loss or gain. No matter what you gain or lose during a conversation, there is always an exchange of knowledge. Many scholars, like Newmark (1988), have speculated that translated texts could generally be improved, hence it is advised that an effort be made to assess a translated book.

5.3. Equivalence in Translation

Because of its close relationship to both the theoretical and practical dimensions of translation, the idea of equivalence has long piqued the interest of translation experts. The concept of equivalence became central to translations schools of thought in the mid-20th century, and it was intended to signify that the original and translated texts are essentially same. Researchers wanted to determine what kind of similarities and patterns in intensity gave rise to various equivalences. In what follows, this section makes an effort to provide a critical analysis of the equivalency paradigm as it has been formulated by the following scholars: Vinay and Darbelnet (1958), Nida and Taber (1969), Catford (1965), House (1997), Newmark (1981), Baker (1992), and Pym (2010).

According to Vinay and Darbelnet (1995, p.255), "complete equivalents" in a bilingual dictionary are a necessary and sufficient requirement for equivalence of phrases between linguistic groups to be accepted. While they acknowledged that statements like these are ideological, they also acknowledged that glossaries and idiom collections are inherently incomplete (p. 256). Thus, it is not sufficient or enough for a good translation to find an analogous terminology in a lexicon or dictionary to a term in the SL text; rather, the context around the phrase in consideration plays an equally vital part in deciding the translation technique chosen. In conclusion, they say that whether or not equivalences need to be created depends on the circumstances. Consequently, translators are urged to consider the ST's perspective first while trying to solve a problem (p. 255).

Consequently, translators are urged to consider the ST's perspective first while trying to solve a problem (p. 255).

According to Nida, there are essentially two kinds of equivalent: formal equivalence and dynamic equivalence. In particular, according to Nida, the goal of formal equivalence is to have the TT closely mirror the ST in form and substance, whereas the goal of evolving equivalence is to have the TT deliver the ST text in the most natural way possible. One may argue that Nida supports dynamic equivalence because he sees it as a more efficient translation process. It should come as no surprise, considering that Nida was attempting to have the same effect on several audiences at once when translating the Bible at the time he proposed his ideas on equivalent. Since it is maintained that "dynamic equivalence in translation" extends beyond the proper transfer of information, Nida's choice is more explicitly expressed in Nida and Taber's edition (1969, p. 25).

House (1997) has developed a translation model based on pragmatic theories of language usage, where the essential condition "for equivalence of ST and TT is that they should correspond in function". Equivalent pragmatic measures should be used to accomplish this purpose. Consequently, the "textual" characteristics as well as functionality of the source must be preserved in order to determine whether or not the translation is of sufficient quality. House has differentiated between "overt translation and covert translation" by conducting contrastive German-English conversation analysis. Overt translation, as the phrase suggests, refers to a TT that has indicators that "betray" its status as a translation. By contrast, a covert translation (TT) performs the same tasks as the source text (ST) because the translator has minimised cultural variations as much as feasible. To sum up, one might say that House's theory is more adaptable than Catford's since it takes into account the pragmatics of translation via the use of real-world instances.

In her seminal work, *In Other Words*, Baker (1997) takes a middle ground on the contentious question of equivalency, arguing that the concept is relative since it is affected by language and cultural contexts. Her work is organised into chapters according to the several levels of equivalence discussed within it, including those of the word, phrase, grammar, text, and pragmatics. Thus, concepts like grammatical, textual, and pragmatic equivalence are discussed. To elaborate, we might say that equivalence at the word level is different from equivalent at the supra-world level. Baker's use of a bottom-up method to translation recognises the significance of individual words throughout the process of translating, because the translator first examines the terms as individual components in order to discover their counterpart in the TL. Baker continues by defining the term word, alluding to its complexity due to the fact that the same word might have multiple meanings in several languages. Therefore, while translating a term, it is important to take into account factors like number, gender, and tense (pp.11-12).

5.4. The Concept of Transparency in Translation

The production of a suitable target text relies heavily on the decisions that the translator makes while they are in the process of translating the source material. They are an important component of interlingual communication and, in a sense, the perspective of the translators themselves. On the other hand, the pursuit of translations that are transparent is an effort to stifle this perspective and appears to be a direct connection to the subservient function that translation has typically played in the past.

The degree to which a translation gives the impression "to a native speaker of the target language that it was originally written in that language and complies with the grammatical, syntactical, and idiomatic norms of that language is referred to as the transparency of the translation" (Munday, 2007, p.63). The criteria for measuring the "transparency of a translation" may be discovered more clearly: idiomatic translations "sound right", while other non-idiomatic translations "sound incorrect" may also be considered transparent. Having said that, a translator may, depending on the circumstances, make a deliberate effort to provide a translation that is word for word. In most cases, literary translators, translator of religious or historical writings, and translators of other types of literature stick as closely as they can to the original text. As a result of this, they often and intentionally push the limits of the target text in order to develop an expression that is not idiomatic.

A transparent translation assures integrity, consonance, and equivalence, and it is just as excellent as the source; for this reason, individuals may claim to have studied Dostoyevsky and Kafka when, in many instances, what they have read "is a translation of their work" (Schaffner, 1999, p.61). The goal of a transparent translation is to produce a text that is easy to read, free of linguistic style, and that, as a result, creates the impression that it is identical to the original. Therefore, in light of such preconceptions, the translators primarily focus on ensuring his or her translation appear as "natural" as possible in order to create an appearance of transparency. This effect is an impression of the source text, something Venuti (1996) does not consider to be a translation any more.

According to Lopez and Wilkinson (2003), the perception of transparency is predicated on two premises: the first is that there is a way to eliminate the differences that exist between languages and cultures, and the second is that all of the possible ways of translating a text can be condensed into a single translation. Hermans (1996, p.5) asserts that the social standing that translations and translators have traditionally been accorded is the root cause of this abstraction. According to Hermans, there has always been a hierarchical distinction between originals and translations, as well as "between authors and translators"; translation, in general, has always been given a lower status. And this has been articulated in stereotypical opposites, such as "original effort vs unoriginal effort, major vs minor, art versus craft". This inferior standing is also shown by the fact that the academic field of translation did not begin to be recognised for its own merits as a distinct field of study till the end of the twentieth century (Munday, 2001).

In addition to the "transparency of the translation", translators and translation theorists need to take into account the "transparency of the translator", whose work is sometimes misattributed or even ignored entirely when it is cited as if it were the original.

5.5. Machine Translation

The development of computerised systems for translating texts from one language to another is often hailed as a significant step forward in the fields of communication and language. However, it is important to question how well texts translated by machines retain the message, style, cultural projection, and social nuances of the original text.

In the realm of Artificial Intelligence, "machine translation" refers to fully automated translation. Automated or machine translation is the use of a computer programme to convert text from one language (the source language) into another (the target language) without the intervention of a human translator. Machine translation aims to automate the process of translating text from one language to another while maintaining the same meaning in both languages. Machine translation, or MT for short, is the practise of producing translated texts via the use of automated techniques, rather than human intervention. Tools that help translators in other ways (such as access to remote vocabularies or online dictionaries, or the transmission and receipt of texts) are not included in this approach (Arnold, 1994).

The term "computer-aided translation" (CAT) can be employed to describe any kind of translation accomplished with the help of a computer. However, the essence of MT lies in automating the whole translation process, thus this distinction must be remembered.

Several suggestions have been suggested by scholars to explain where the concept of machine translation first came from (Bareten, 2019). Some researchers think that the advancement of machine translation may be traced back to the 9th-century activity "of Al-Kindi, an Arabic cryptographer" who developed methods for translating very difficult languages (Slocum, 1988). Current machine translation takes use of all of these methods, which Arnold (1994, p.51) claims Al-Kindi pioneered "cryptanalysis, frequency analysis, probability, and statistics".

Machine translation has come a long way in recent years, with the advent of multilingual translation apps for both Android and iOS like DeepL. The translation results have been evaluated critically, with an emphasis on how closely they match the intended meaning and the underlying semantic structure of the original texts. Measured in terms of authenticity, fidelity, or extent of integrity degradation, this metric is used to determine how well a machine translation's results come to reflecting the original author's meaning.

Both rule-based and corpus-based methods are used for machine translation. While rules are automatically derived from a corpus in the corpus-based method, rules are defined by human experts in rule-based machine translation.

Several methods for translating texts automatically exist. There are benefits and drawbacks to each machine translation method. It seems that what one method has, the other method is missing, and vice versa. While the statistical technique makes only cursory or no reference to grammar, rule-based approaches actively seek to comprehend the underlying rules of a given language. Computational linguists have been using rule-based machine translation systems since they were invented. A human agent's participation is crucial to this strategy since it is the human operator that establishes the rules. This means that people draw on their own experiences and education when drafting the regulations. This method's strength lies in its ability to do syntactic and, to some degree, semantic analysis of the input.

The main drawback of "rule-based machine translation" is that it takes a lot of effort and in-depth linguistics expertise to construct the rules. Last but not least, it would be quite difficult to record every rule. But from a syntactic perspective, the rule-based approach is invaluable for machine translation. Continuous improvements are possible with rule-based machine translation since problematic rules may be identified and corrected. For languages without an existing parallel bilingual corpus, this method may serve as a solid foundation.

5.6. The Concept of Terminology in Translation

Terminology involves the investigation of technical topics and the words used to describe them. These domain-specific knowledge chunks were created via the collaboration and exchange of a small but dedicated group of language community specialists. In the field of Terminology, experts describe the structures of specialised knowledge and the means by which that information is disseminated in various settings of interaction. Term bases, dictionaries, and glossaries are all examples of terminological resources that may be utilised for both text decoding and text production, and their creation is an integral part of the process. As one of the variables that impacts translation quality, the sufficiency of the terminology employed in a text and its appropriateness in the understanding capacity of message recipients is directly connected to terminology, both from a theoretical and an applied standpoint. In this sense, terminological issues are often seen as a challenge in translation that has to be tackled and resolved throughout the translation process. This necessitates translators of technical materials to be secret terminologists, with the ability to engage in terminological operations as a way of information gathering. For this reason, it is essential that they have considerable expertise in the application of translation technology, computer tools, and internet materials. Thus, expert translators must be familiar with how to make the most of all available tools in order to effectively address terminological issues throughout the evaluation and interpretation of the source text, and during the creation as well as modification of the target language text.

Both concepts of Translation and Terminology, as Cabré (2004) explains, have their origins in the pragmatic activities of responding to information and communication demands via practical means. Both pursuits have the trait of being interdisciplinary and serve as areas of convergence for the study of language, cognition, and communication (Cabré, 2004). But they are distinct in that terminology is not a form of communication but rather a tool for that purpose. To facilitate the interlingual transference of terminological elements and the information they contain, terminology is essential for the translator even if translation is mainly concerned with the communication process. There are four levels of terminology participation in translation work, as outlined by Cabré (2004). In the first, passive stage, the translator looks for an answer by consulting various sources. As a second step, translators may utilise their lexical expertise to suggest a neologism to be used in the target language. As shown at third step, translators play the role of arbitrary terminologists by identifying the gap in the field's conceptual framework and proposing a new term based on established patterns of word development. At the fourth and final stage, translators use their own datasets, which contain words from previous translations, to find solutions to difficulties.

Specialized terminology and terminological phrasemes provide the greatest challenge to translators in terms of both syntactic and semantic complexities when working with a specialised material. Understanding the meaning of these words in their original context in the text is thus essential. Term extraction occurs after term identification has been completed in a translation project. Both need picking out words from the original text in order to run some kind of analysis on them, translate them, and then maintain and construct a "terminology" for a certain field. There are benefits and downsides to both human and automated word extraction, but in practise, most translators choose to undertake the task manually.

Translators also need to know how to apply the terminology they've gleaned from texts in context and make connections between those phrases and real-world notions. Primary access keywords, synonyms, variations, phraseological units, etc., are some of the many ways that words may be organised. Grammar, use, and equivalency are all examples of data categories associated with terms, whereas definition, explanation, context, and figure are all examples of data categories associated with concepts.

When translating technical documents, terminological variety is a major source of difficulty. Having numerous possible synonyms for the same technical idea makes it difficult to choose the one that works best in the given textual and linguistic setting. It is not uncommon for translators to use a synonym instead of the precise match provided by a specialist dictionary. Rarely do dictionaries contain information regarding collocational constraints while listing a number of possible choices. Because of this, translators need to have the standards to take the right decision. The existence of many linguistic labels for the same idea is an example of denominative variety. There is usually not a one-to-one relationship between denominative variations across languages, therefore understanding their origins and the variational parameters to which they are sensitive is essential. The study of terminological variation is valuable because it may provide light on the fluidity of conceptualization and the variety of communication settings in which concepts are used.

5.7. Technical Translation

Technical translation is essential in many fields, but especially in academia, where it serves as a conduit for the exchange of ideas between researchers from diverse cultural backgrounds. It is also useful for detecting instances of plagiarism in the classroom. Problems with lexical and syntactical accuracy are the most common in this kind of translation.

The scope of technical translation extends beyond the translation of scientific and technological materials to include other fields, such as economics and medical. Expertise in the field and familiarity with the appropriate vocabulary are seen as prerequisites for the translation of such works. There is a belief that a technical translator just needs a thorough understanding of specialized terminology and a willingness to swap words for words in the target language. The universal goal of translation is to facilitate communication, hence there are parallels across the many fields that use this technique. What this implies is that, literary translation and technical translation have some common ground. There is more to translating technical literature for the workplace or scientific communication than just knowing the appropriate vocabulary. Culture and history shape not just how we talk to one another but also the fields we study and the forms of writing we use. There are major issues in translating technical materials, especially at the levels of vocabulary.

It's no secret that academia has always looked down on technical translation as "the ugly duckling of translation". Unlike other varieties, this one lacks the flair and cachet to make it a desirable option. As a subset of the larger translation industry, technical translation is sometimes looked down upon as nothing more than a specialised vocabulary and topic knowledge quiz. Some people see technical translation with the same level of suspicion as they would a modern-day barbarian because of these qualities, especially topic knowledge.

It is evident that, historically speaking, technical translation has been considered the second-rate relative of "genuine" translation. The literature on translation theory has generally ignored this kind of translation, which is common in the vocational and industrial sectors.

The transmission of information across different languages and cultures is known as technical translation. The vocabulary of a certain area is used in technical writing. Consequently, technical translation is a subset of specialised translation that entails the translation of transcripts written by technical writers (owner's manuals, user guides, etc.) or, more narrowly, texts that pertain to technological subject areas.

It is important to accurately describe technological processes, translate technical words, and adhere to a suitable presentation style while working on a technical translation project. Technical documents, such as how-to guides for new pieces of software or hardware, must be translated by a person with a high level of language and professional expertise.

Aside from the prerequisite knowledge for translating technical documents, it is crucial that the translator has professional competence and skill in the fields to which the technical documentation pertains. Professional, highly-qualified professionals in the industry, the translators we engage have the requisite specialization in technical translations. Basic technical translation services are carried out by professionals who have extensive theoretical and practical knowledge of the relevant subjects, as a majority of professional "translators and editors" are themselves experts in different domains of production. There are professional technical translators in the necessary fields, beginning with those with essential technical specialization and finishing with specialists who hold scientific titles and degrees, to ensure that the translations adhere to the specific terminology for subsequent proofreading as well as editing of translations.

Works Cited

Arnold, M. (1994) On Translating Homer, London: AMS Press.

Baker, M. (1992) In Other Words: A Coursebook on Translation, London and New York: Routledge.

Baker, M. (1997) The Routledge Encyclopedia of Translation Studies, London and New York: Routledge.

Catford, J. C. (1965) A Linguistic Theory of Translation, London: Oxford University Press (1965). (See also Catford, J. C. "Translation shifts", in The Translation Studies Reader, L. Venuti (ed.) London: Routledge. pp. 141–147.)

Hermans, T. (1996) "Norms and the Determination of Translation: A Theoretical Framework", in Translation, Power, Subversion, R. Alvarez and M. C-A Vidal Claramonte (eds.) Clevedon: Multilingual Matters. pp. 25–51.

House, J. (1997) Translation Quality Assessment: A Model Revisited, Tübingen: Gunter Narr.

Munday, J. (2001) Introducing Translation Studies: Theories and Applications, London and New York: Routledge, 1st edition.

Munday, J. (2007) "Translation and Ideology: A Textual Approach", The Translator, *13*(2) 195–217.

Newmark, P. (1988). A Textbook of Translation, New York and London: Prentice Hall.

Nida, E. A. (1964) Toward a Science of Translating, Leiden: E. J. Brill.

Nida, E. A. and C. R. Taber (1969) The Theory and Practice of Translation, Leiden: E. J. Brill.

Pym, A. (2010) "On Toury's Laws of how Translators Translate", in Beyond Descriptive Translation Studies: Investigations in homage to Gideon Toury, A. Pym, M. Shlesinger and D. Simeoni (eds) Amsterdam and Philadelphia: John Benjamins.

Schäffner, C. (1998) "Skopos theory", in Routledge Encyclopedia of Translation Studies, M. Baker (ed.) London: Routledge. pp. 235–238.

Venuti, L. (1996) The Translator's Invisibility: A History of Translation, London and New York: Routledge.

Vinay, J. P. and J. Darbelnet (1958/1977) Stylistique Comparée du Français et de L'anglais: Méthode de Traduction, Paris: Didier, 2nd edition.

Vinay, J. P. and J. Darbelnet (1995) Comparative Stylistics of French and English: A Methodology for Translation, trans. by J. C. Sager and M. J. Hamel (eds.) Amsterdam and Philadelphia, PA: John Benjamins.

CHAPTER SIX

APPLIED TRANSLATION: EXPLORING THE NEW TRENDS

6.1. Introduction

Translation theory and practice have always been described as fundamental components of applied linguistics. Researchers in translation theories have explored the attempt by modern translators to share core translation activities between human and machine translators. The narrative is to explicate ways in which artificial intelligence could assist human translators in the translation process since the new trends in the translation are focused on the use of technology. This chapter explores fundamental issues in recognition of translation as an applied discipline from the purview of the focus on technology in translation.

6.2. Translation as an Applied Discipline

Studies have attempted to escalate the discussion of what does "applied" mean in the field of Applied Translation? Researchers from a variety of fields have offered their perspectives on a topic referred to as Applied Translation. Historically, Holmes distinguished between "pure" translation studies from "applied" translation (Holmes 2000, p.176). The applied branch addresses issues pertaining to "translation's use". The practice of translating documents with the assistance of computers is referred to as "machine translation". It has a lengthy history, several different techniques and architectures, four fundamental categories, some closely similar concepts, and some disadvantages.

When we talk about the practical application of research and investigation in any field, we are referring to what we mean when we say that field is "applied". When referring to Translation Studies, the term "applied" refers to the procedure of translation being carried out for the sake of a particular goal and with a particular audience in mind. When presenting the completed, useable translated text, a certain level of precision and quality is typically maintained throughout the process. The translation of scientific research into numerous languages, for instance, in order to facilitate their use in collaborative environments and ubiquitous access, is one area of applied translation.

Translation practices which discuss a specific objective as well as a specialized (category of) end user(s) and that indicate performing an action for or about translation in accordance with some standards of quality are the focus of Applied Translation Studies, which is the performative subdivision of Translation Studies. Applied Translation Studies is preoccupied with translation operations that take into account a specialized purpose. Applied Translation is a designation given to fields that pertain in part to Translation Studies and in part to other disciplines. Some examples of these fields include translators training and education, translation resources, and translation critiques, amongst others.

The field of Applied Translation Studies is therefore subdivided into four distinct subfields according to Holmes' system. The first issue is instruction for translators, which is most likely the most significant topic of concern. The second one is the generation of translating tools such as "lexicographical" and terminology reference books and grammatical structures that are customized to meet the requirements of translators. The third category is the development of translation strategy, and the work of the translation researcher in this area is to deliver educated counsel to others in determining the position and function of translation services and translators to humanity. The final one is translation critiques, which typically has a very poor standard and is, in many countries, largely unaffected by recent advances in translation theory (Shuttleworth & Cowie, 2014).

One area of applied translation that have evolved over the years and remained relevant in contemporary discourses in translation is the application of technology in translation, which can be discussed under the umbrella of Machine Translation (MT). According to Holmes (2002), the recognition of machine translation within the generality of applied translation is premised on the projection of the concept of "use", how computer or technology is used to facilitate or translate texts. It is thus pertinent to escalate the discussion of machine translation, focusing mainly on areas machine translation have assisted human translators in the process of providing suitable and contextually driven equivalents to the original texts.

6.3. Machine Translation: How Humans and Computers Function in Translation

Machine translation, also known as MT, is a tool that helps human translators make better use of their time. A human translator may use a Machine Translation system and then physically edit its translation to rectify any errors found. On the other hand, there is no assurance that a particular translated portion generated by the Machine translation system will be of sufficient quality for post-editing. To determine whether or not to retain the portion in the final translation, a human translator might have to peruse it several times before reaching a conclusion. The outcome of this procedure cannot be reliably predicted, and it is also very inefficient in terms of producing texts that do not require the editing services of a human translator.

New technologies have had a profound impact on translation and are currently shaping both its research and theoretical development, despite the fact that they do not introduce a novel theoretical framework (Munday, 2008). Recently, there has been a rise in the demand for translation services as a result of the growing importance of interregional collaboration and the need to share information. The majority of the content requires translation. Most of this activity is monotonous and repetitious, requiring precision and consistency in performance, while some aspects are challenging and difficult. It is becoming increasingly challenging for skilled translators to keep up with the growing demand for translation. In this particular circumstance, the utilization of machine translation has proven to be of tremendous assistance (Chéragui, 2012).

The generality of the process of translating written documents using computer algorithms is attributed to as machine translation (MT). In most cases, it is included alongside computer-aided translation under the umbrella term of computer translation, which refers to translation that is performed using a computer. The degree to which a human translator is involved in the process is one of the criteria that is used to categorize computer-aided translation. Other criteria include if the program gives conventional or personalized translation and what kind of system architecture or strategy is utilized (Baker & Saldanha, 2009).

Unassisted machine translation, also known as completely automated MT, refers to the process in which computer systems translate an entire document without the assistance of human operators. Since the entire text is evaluated in a single operation, these systems are also referred to as "batch" systems in some circles. The two components of automated machine translation are human assisted machine translation (HAMT) and "machine assisted human translation" (MAHT). Human translators participate in the process of human-assisted machine translation (also known as HAMT or interactive MT) to address issues of uncertainty in the source text (ST) or to select the most appropriate word or sentence from the target language (TL) for output. In the MAHT approach, human translators are assisted by computer algorithms as they conduct the translation process. CAT, also known as machine assisted human translation, is a type of MAHT that is gaining in popularity (Baker & Saldanha, 2009).

MT can also be categorized in accordance with the field of study for which it was developed to translate. Generic machine translation systems are systems that have been designed to translate documents across all subject groups or disciplines. Systems that are tailored to particular user groups and designed for a unique function are known as special purpose or customized systems (Baker & Saldanha, 2009). Thus, It's possible for a MT system to be tailored to translate in a particular domain, such as physics, chemistry, mathematics, biology, psychology or politics, for instance.

The classification of MT systems also takes into account the number of languages that are being translated as well as the direction in which the translation is going. Computer algorithms can be developed for either two or more languages (multilingual systems) or for just two languages (bilingual systems). Computer algorithms that are bilingual can be constructed to function in either one direction only (unidirectional) or in both paths simultaneously (bidirectional).

The use of machine translation is a very beneficial tool for the instruction of translators. Throughout the course of the lesson, the instructor is required to display numerous examples of writings that have been transcribed. Using MT to complete such a work will be both quicker and simpler. Teachers are able to demonstrate the distinctions between human and computer skills and capabilities by utilizing MT in their classrooms. A significant number of vocabularies and/or documents that have been translated are typically saved within an MT system. Both instructors and students will benefit from using these, as they will make it easier to look up terms in dictionaries and differentiate between correctly formed and incorrectly formed grammatical structures.

Translators can benefit greatly from the use of machine translation. The translator will have access to all different kinds of textual and terminological resource books as a result of this. The use of translation tools provided by MT comes with a number of benefits. The search for the necessary information can be completed more quickly and with less effort. The translators can get information that is up to date due to this resource. It enables the user to explore multiple vocabularies at the same time.

Technological translation tools take up less space physically and are simpler to carry and store than their analog counterparts.

It has been brought to user 's attention that among the many duties of the translator is the formulation of translation strategy. In addition, MT is involved in this task. A translator needs to be aware of the significant function that MT plays in the modern society. He ought to point out that MT makes translation easier, speeds up communications, and prompts an increase in the amount of research and development carried out in a variety of fields, including the computer, machine learning, and internet businesses. In the realm of translation policy, efforts are made to demonstrate that automated translation is neither a competitor nor an adversary to human translators.

6.4. Machine Translator and Human Translator: in Competition or Complementation?

The question of if the machine translation could well substitute or work in conjunction with human translator is one that has garnered a lot of attention in recent discussions on developments and shifts in the function of technology in translation. Researchers such as Dia (2022) are among those who have asserted that even though MT has had a substantial influence on translation, human translation efforts will not be supplanted by Machine Translators and will proceed to be present in the years to come. Because MT is nevertheless a far from being an indispensable component of any literary translation exercise, Şahin et al. (2021) came to the conclusion that translators' connections with Machine Translator and pessimistic perceptions against it may transform in a favorable manner as MT continues to advance and translation practice continues to develop. Nevertheless, Maghsoudi and Mirzaeian (2020) assert that MT has reached a stage where it is now capable of competing with human translators. This is consistent with the findings of the study conducted by Farahani (2020), which came to the conclusion that machine translations (MTs) were proficient translations after discovering a lack of proportionally considerable distinction between machine and human translation.

The processing of an appropriate as well as satisfactory translated version that produces the text of the SL into the TT has always been a primary concern for human translators (Gerber, 2012). This is because the process of translation takes up a significant amount of their time. Because of this, machine translation, which is the process of translating information in one language into another with the assistance of software, has made its way into our everyday existence. Because of the dramatic increase in the volume of international communication over the past few years, the standard of MT services has significantly increased (Li et al., 2014). To put it another way, contemporary MT services such as "Google Translate and Bing Translator" have taken important steps in the direction of enabling users to comprehend material written in different languages (Almutawa and Izwaini, 2015).

In comparison to MT, human translation possesses a few distinguishing qualities that set it apart. To begin, the pace at which human translation is ordinarily carried out is typically much slower than that at which MTs are carried out. In addition, human translations are reviewed by humans, whether the translator or the proofreader.

It is a common belief that the best way to evaluate MT is to compare it to highly skilled translations (Papineni et al., 2002).

The first of these sentiments was articulated as early as 1951 in a review that J.E. Holmstrom wrote for the United Nations Educational, Scientific, and Cultural Organization (UNESCO). He was of the opinion that the literary style that would be produced by a machine translation (MT) mechanism "would be appalling and richer of 'errors' and deceptive meanings compared to the worst that any human translator generates". The reason for this was because, according to Holmstrom (1951), "translation is a craft; one which at each phase involves individual preference between un-codifiable different options; not simply straightforward transpositions of conflated pairs of signifiers but selections of attributes relying for their worthiness in relation to the contingent learning and charisma of the translator". His remarks, which were based entirely on supposition and came three years before the first preliminary exhibition of a modest conceptual model, anticipated the event by that amount of time. In spite of this, similar remarks have been made over and over by translators for the past nearly half a century.

The second outlook is one that has carried on right up until the current day. However, there is currently no question that computer-based translation mechanisms are not competitors to human translators; rather, they are helpful tools that empower human translators to improve their efficiency in the field of specialized translation, or they facilitate ways of translating content that no human translator would have ever strived to translate before. Within the scope of this discussion, we must differentiate:

i.   machine translation (MT), which intends to handle the entirety of the translation process but produces results that must inevitably be amended;

ii. computer assists for translators, also known as translation tools, which provide assistance to professional translators; and

iii. translation algorithms for "occasional" non-translator users, which only generate preliminary versions to assist understanding and are not intended to replace professional translators.

It wasn't until the mid-1990s that these distinctions were brought to light. In the past, people have believed that MT systems, regardless of whether they were operating on a supercomputer or a microprocessor, were capable of performing all of these activities to a greater or lesser degree of success. The inability to recognize unique demands and also to configure systems that specifically fulfill them has facilitated, at least in part, to the proliferation of false assumptions regarding translation technology and the effect it has on human translators, Particularly, the inability to design processes specifically to meet these different needs.

When the initially released models of Machine translation emerged for personal computers (in the mid-1990s), it was generally believed that they would ultimately be utilized in a comparable way as the large computer processes had been, i.e. either to generate "rough" (unexpurgated) editions for information purposes, or "draft translations" for later modification and sophistication. This assumption was based on the fact that it was widely believed that the mainframe structures had been used in much the same way. It was also widely assumed that the primary beneficiaries of MT production would be translators or at least individuals who had extensive expertise of both the source language and the target language. In the case of large organizations, it was anticipated that the majority of the translators would be professionally trained translators.

However, by the late 1980s – and at an accelerating rate since the early 1990s – developments on a number of fronts flipped this framework and its underlying assumptions on their heads. These translator workstations are primarily computer translation tools and are not meant to create even incomplete translations fully automatically. They were created especially for the use of human translators and have become commercially available in recent years. Firstly, there has been the accessibility of translator workstations developed exclusively to be utilized by human translators. In spite of the fact that a number of highly qualified translators have acquired personal computer (PC) systems and have been able to use them effectively – a number of systems are designed specifically for this market – other professional translators have opted to make use of workstations, which are becoming more reasonably priced for independent translators. Second, an ever-increasing number of people who have no interest in translation as such have purchased and started using PC-based systems. These systems are being used solely as "aids for communication", which means that the content of the texts that are being translated is of much less significance. Thirdly, the expansion of global telecommunication connections and the Internet, which have made instant communication in a variety of languages possible, has resulted in an increasing need for translation platforms and services that are able to deal quickly and in real time with an enormous volume of electronic texts of varying kinds (including published articles, electronic mail, and conversations in chatrooms). Finally, the increased accessibility of databases and other information resources written in a variety of languages (again, primarily on the Internet) has created a demand for bilingual search and access devices that come equipped with translation modules (for translating search terms and/or translating abstracts or summarizing, for example).

As such, where does that leave the expert translator in light of these changes? It makes sense to classify requests for translation into three broad categories. The first category includes the time-honored need for high-quality versions suitable for publication. The second type, "translation for absorption", emerged with the information boom of the 20th century and involves the need for copies of papers with a brief lifespan in order to collect and analyze data. The third category is translation for human contact, which is a novel type of on-the-spot translation (the conventional function of the translator) brought about by electronic technology.

As a whole, the effectiveness of large-scale MT systems in the field of translation for wide distribution has been uneven. Translators typically work in one of these methods. Lacking some command over the source language makes it difficult to use the comparatively low-quality output, which needs to be amended by human translators, in a cost-effective manner. Only the bigger global corporations with stockpiles of paperwork that can't be processed any other way have had the resources to consider outsourcing even a portion of their documentation processes. These systems are both expensive to create (for example, by compiling extensive dictionaries of company or industry terms) and expensive to maintain, as they are essentially company-specific (or at least subject-specific), such as "post-editors, technical and linguistic personnel" Skilled translators' participation has been inconsistent (some have post-editing experience), but these trends have largely emerged independently of the translation industry.

Translation platforms have emerged as a practical and, arguably, more alluring option for professional translators in recent years, allowing for more efficient production of publishable-quality versions in keeping with translators' established practices. Such platforms have hitherto been rare outside of big corporations and a few translation firms. The majority of expert translators will likely be utilizing such tools in the near future, not only out of business necessity, but also out of a desire to improve their own work experience.

In the past, skilled translators rarely worked on texts intended for cultural adaptation. In businesses, secretaries and other administrative workers with a passing familiarity with languages have traditionally handled this job on an as-needed basis and under considerable time constraints. Since the people doing the job are not experts, they are understandably frustrated by the outcomes. Since the first MT systems became accessible in the 1970s, they have served a necessary purpose. Authorities at the European Commission's use of Systran exemplifies the worth of such "partial" translation tools. By a wide margin, the integration purposes of machine translation (MT) outweigh its production and distribution translation purposes. The most common purpose cited for the more affordable PC-based machine translation is knowledge absorption, both individually and corporately. Skilled translators almost never encounter such results. There will undoubtedly be an ever-increasing need for translation services like these. No one in the translation industry has really dabbled in this before, and it's not likely to change any time soon.

The scope of translation for interpersonal interactions extends to both verbal (talk) and written (letters, emails) forms of interaction between human beings. Translators have been and will continue to be used on occasion by their organizations for a variety of purposes, including but not limited to acting as translators for international guests and mediating between parties in internal communications. However, the translator cannot play a part in the translation of electronic communications in real time; instead, completely automated systems must be used for this task.

However, the availability of online automated translation services is likely to bring to light the significance of translation as an integral part of worldwide communication to an unprecedented degree. Eventually, translation will be held in much greater regard than in the past. Individuals who rely on the rudimentary results of Machine translation will eventually appreciate the superior quality of human-edited versions. For this reason, it's safe to assume that the need for human-made translation will increase, making the translation industry busy than ever before. For their part, expert translators will have access to a variety of computer-based translation tools that will help them boost output and ensure the highest standards of accuracy. In sum, translators need not worry about the impending rise of mechanization and MT; instead, they stand to gain from an increased business and better working conditions.

6.5. Current Trends in Technology and Translation

The environment we live in is undergoing such rapid transformation that Artificial Intelligence (AI) and other forms of innovative technology have begun to have an impact in the fields of linguistics and translation, which may result in a shift in the market for translation services. It is not possible to deny the truth that the translation business is a vibrant one. The manner in which things are done will continue to be influenced by and altered by new technological patterns as they emerge. Businesses have a responsibility to adapt to more recent changes and stay current with the latest trends and projections in the field of translation.

It should come as no surprise to anyone working in the translation industry that significant shifts are taking place in the translation of official documents. Even though the transformations might not be nearly as readily apparent to people who work in the field of specialized writing or who compose or study literature and poetry, those fields are still being impacted by the shifts. The process of delivering documents, particularly specialized documents, in a number of different language variants is being sped up as a result of these adjustments. As a result of this, the occupations of scientific communication and translation are undergoing significant shifts and are increasingly converging into a single field (Gnecchi et al. 2011). What is the driving force behind these shifts? And what is it that is luring the funds that is then used to accelerate these processes? At its core, it can be boiled down to the requirements of the information economy. Since a decade ago, businesses that wanted to market their goods and services in nations such as Switzerland, Belgium, or Canada were required to customize their offerings and transform them into a predetermined number of different languages. Now, however, because of the trade agreements that were established in the 1990s and the subsequent expansion in trade that resulted in the creation of a truly global marketplace, businesses located anywhere in the world have an incentive to promote their products everywhere; in order to do so, they need to adapt their goods and services to be compatible with the local cultural and language differences.

The practice of translation is acquiring an ever-greater level of significance in the modern world. These days, a significant number of businesses as well as organizations disseminate and communicate their material in a variety of languages.

A sector with an approximated value of $39.37 trillion at the present time. Since it is anticipated that the market will expand at a cumulative yearly rate of expansion of 2.07% between the years 2021 and 2028, the market for translation services is anticipated to be valued $46.22 by the end of the forecast period.

Translation is one of the many fields that is heavily impacted by technology in today's world; this is not an exception. One distinguishing feature of technology is that it is notoriously difficult to anticipate. It is becoming nearly impossible to predict how technology will advance and, as a result, how businesses that are connected to it will develop. Nevertheless, if there is only one method to forecast the future, it would be to evaluate current technological developments and the way they are employed to the Translation business.

The industry of artificial intelligence (AI) has indeed been experiencing consistent growth over the past few years. This momentum is continuing to build, as evidenced by the introduction of cutting-edge services that are propelled by AI in a variety of fields, and the realization among industry specialists that this trend will persist. There is no way to refute the claim that artificial intelligence (AI) has made substantial strides in the past few years. There have been a number of significant breakthroughs in the field of artificial intelligence, including natural language processing (NLP) and machine learning techniques, as well as a wider understanding and implementation of AI. There is little doubt that artificial intelligence will continue its quick development well beyond the year 2023.

It is undeniable that the field of machine translation is experiencing a renaissance as a direct result of the advent of the AI transformation brought about by machine learning. The current status of machine translation within the field of artificial intelligence is not even close to being optimal (Kong, 2022), but when combined with the expertise of humans, it may be possible to produce interpretations that are both speedier and more effective. It is possible that using a translation machine will make the complete translation process more effective, just as narrating this writing would have been quicker than coding it. Although the currently available machine translation algorithms are sufficient for conveying the general meaning of a document, they are lacking in a number of other areas, including adaptability, the ability to comprehend context, and subtleties of expression. Concerns have also been raised regarding the inability of current AI translation tools to provide an accurate approximation of the emotional, social, cultural, environmental, and aesthetic complexity of the original text.

Research have continued to appear in the field of machine translation, and these studies have included replicable breakthroughs in machine learning as well as the general applicability of AI in translation. The scope of research on the application of artificial intelligence to translation has broadened to include a variety of subtopics, such as AI in translation and foreign language instruction, activities related to commercial translation, and so on.

One study that was conducted not too long ago looked at the relationship between the prospective applications of machine translation and the intrinsic challenges it presents (Kong, 2022). The importance of machine translation as a research challenge in natural language processing (NLP) was also investigated in this study. The research was conducted in both the academic and commercial sectors of NLP. According to Kong, in the aftermath of the transformation of artificial intelligence, deep learning is breathing new energy into machine translation.

Kirov and Malamin (2022) carried out research that resulted in the production of tangible data on the subject of artificial intelligence in translation, with the goal of answering the question of whether or not AI in translation poses a danger to human translators. The purpose of the authors' observational sociocultural research was to gain a better understanding of the feelings that Bulgarian translators have regarding AI and its consequences for their line of work. According to the results of their research, it appears that the overwhelming majority of human translators questioned viewed AI and technology as competitive challenges to their profession. They anticipate that human translators will be able to concentrate more on the artistic elements of the work, while digital technology and AI will streamline the more technical aspects of the job. The survey that Kirov and Malamin (2022) conducted may serve as a jumping off point for future research into the impact artificial intelligence has had on a variety of artistic endeavors. In addition, a more recent book by Urlaud and Dessein (2022) synthesizes thorough studies on the role that machine translation plays in educational linguistics. The findings of their study, which acknowledged the difficulties that MT tools encounter when challenged with socio-culturally complicated source material, might help clear the way for the implementation of MT-based instructional aids.

To that extent, there are few significant trends in machine translation that further valid the discussion of translation from the perspective of applied discipline. Where do you see the translation industry going in the years ahead? This is, as usual, an extremely broad and intricate subject. In any case, this segment may help readers see the future more clearly as it may be molded by discussing the Top 3 technological advancements in the translation business:

1. An Analysis of the Four Different Models of Machine Translation

The term "machine translation" has always referred to a process that is completely automated and makes use of artificial intelligence in order to automatically transform a document from one language to another language of the user's choosing. This procedure is entirely computerized and automatic, with no involvement from a human being whatsoever. For the purpose of translating a text, machine translation examines all text components of the text that is being requested as input and recognizes how words influence one another.

There are four distinct approaches to machine translation that are in use today; here are some of the resources available to learn more about them:

1.1. A Form of Automated Translation Based on Rules (RBMT)

The "Classical Technique" is the name given to this particular form of machine translation. It does this by translating documents using grammatical principles and vocabularies that cover all of the most important semantic, morphological, and structural attributes of every language in turn. Rule-based computer translation systems can be broken down into one of three distinct categories:

i. A Computer That Relies on a Compendium Translation
   Obtains a written input and converts it into a product by adhering to the fundamental guidelines outlined in a straightforward vocabulary.
ii. A Mechanism That is Transfer Based Translation
   The input text is analyzed to establish its language structures, the resulting structure is transferred to a structure that is appropriate for the target language, and finally, the translated text that was produced as a result is generated. This method divides the translation process into three steps.
iii. Translation by Means of Interlingual Machines
   In this method, the text that is to be translated from its original language into another language is first rendered into an interlingua, which is a representation that is abstract and independent of language. The interlingua is used as a starting point for the generation of the target language.
iv. Translation by Multilingual Computer Programs
   In this method, the text that is to be translated from its original language into another language is first rendered into an interlingua, which is a representation that is abstract and independent of

language. The interlingua is used as a starting point for the generation of the target language.

2. Translation by means of "statistical machine translation" (SMT)

The production of statistical models for use in statistical machine translation is the primary emphasis of statistical machine translation. These statistical models can be constructed from the examination of massive quantities of either bidirectional (source and destination languages) or monolingual data (target language). This information is referred to as (bilingual or monolingual) text libraries, and it is constructed by conducting an analysis of previously completed human interpretations. During the process of creating text libraries, certain statistical weights are also established. These weights are later utilized in the process of determining the translation that is most likely to be correct.

Following the development of the models, a statistical distribution is applied to the data in order to determine the output that is most likely to correspond to the given input. A machine that is based on rules Word-based techniques are utilized in translation. On the other hand, the vast majority of contemporary SMT algorithms are phrase-based. The goal of phrase-based translation is to alleviate some of the restrictions enforced by word-based translation by translating whole sequences of words, where the durations of the individual words can vary. Phrases are sequences of words that have been generated by a computer. These phrases are not necessarily grammatical phrases; rather, they are phrases that have been collected from multilingual text collections by using statistical techniques.

3. Computer translation using a hybrid approach

A method known as hybrid machine translation is a strategy that integrates a number of different machine translation approaches into a singular system. Because no single strategy can accomplish optimum precision on its own, this approach was developed as a solution to the problem. The use of hybrid machine translation systems is becoming increasingly common as a result of their efficiency in improving translation precision and their prevalence in popular machine translation systems. There are a number of distinct varieties of hybrid machine translation, including Multi-Engine, Statistical Rule Generation, Multi-pass, and Confidence-Based. We will not go into detail describing the different types of hybrid machine translation because it is a very complicated subject; however, please feel free to check out the accompanying article on the

Varieties of Hybrid Machine Translation for more information in-depth than what we are able to provide here.

4. Neural Machine Translation

A method known as Neural Machine Translation teaches itself new languages and automatically translates text using artificial intelligence. One method of automatic translation is superior to another with regard to the performance of a specific work. The translation of writings that deal with subject matter in the fields of medicine, banking, law, and science require a certain level of knowledge in the particular field. This level of expertise is something that translation algorithms are unable to provide at this time. According to the most recent numbers available, the market for machine translation is presently valued at a total of $800 million. The market for machine translation is anticipated to achieve a valuation of $7.5 trillion by the year 2030, assuming an average yearly growth rate of 30% from now until then.

The process of translating our writings using machine translation is rapidly advancing, and as a result, it is becoming more intelligent and accurate. Because of the anticipated numbers and the expansion of the market, computers will continue to advance in the future years in order to accurately interpret difficult texts.

There are also other trends that are anticipated to emerge in the field of applied translation. These trends are primarily centered on the question of how to make better use of other aspects of a variety of fields in order to enhance translation operations. The following are some of the patterns that are expected in the future:

a. A search approach for multiple languages
   SEO (search engine optimization), also known as multilingual SEO, refers to a technique that optimizes the material of a website for numerous languages. The implementation of a multinational SEO strategy results in the development of a more comprehensive computerized business policy that is aimed at multiple languages and, as a result, a larger audience. This is an approach with the primary goal of improving the performance of country-specific material.
   An increasing number of businesses are working to extend their internet footprint across international borders. A Search approach that employs multiple languages is not only highly adaptable, but also extremely cost-effective. Additionally, not only will the number

of people who visit your website increase, but so will their level of satisfaction. The manner in which people utilize the internet varies greatly from nation to nation. As a result, it is essential to keep various factors in mind when employing a strategy for SEO that takes into account multiple languages.

The implementation of a multinational SEO strategy is now feasible thanks to recent advancements and techniques. Consider the benefits it can offer to organizations as well as the experiences it provides for consumers (or customers). It is expected that in the not too distant future, it will become increasingly normal for businesses to follow a digital marketing strategy that concentrates on numerous languages rather than just one.

a. A technology known as video remote translating, or VRI

The technology known as video remote translating makes it possible for sign language translators to communicate with deaf or hard of hearing individuals who are located in the same location. Therefore, there is no requirement for the presence of a translator at the location in order to translate the communication. The Virtual Reality Translating (VRI) technology fills the void that previously existed between on-site translating services and telephone translating services. This is due to the fact that the new technology makes it feasible to interact with the individual in question whenever it is necessary, thereby eradicating the need for an on-site translation whenever one is required. The use of "video remote translating technology" carries a number of benefits, the most significant of which are as follows:

– Conversations that are easier to follow for anyone and everyone involved.

– It is possible to incorporate contextual and non-verbal cues, and doing so is cost-effective. It results in significant cost reductions.

– Can be used either upon desire or upon suggestion.

Because most of the testing for this technology took place during the COVID-19 epidemic, it is still in the early stages of development. It possesses a multitude of benefits, including those that pertain to the activities that we participate in on a daily basis. For instance, it is becoming more typical for activities such as going to school or working to take place virtually; consequently, the future looks promising for VRI. The development of translation technology is just getting started, but it will undoubtedly continue to advance in the future.

6.6. Basic Branches of Applied Translation

Beyond the discussion of applied translation from the academic perspective, which involves producing articles to escalate the areas translation have been applied and used to enhance communication, there are known areas or branches of applied statistics, as seen in the diagram below taken from Toury (1995).

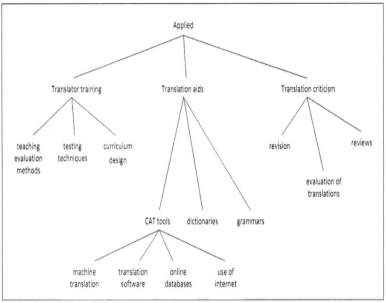

(taken from Toury, 1995)

The diagram above provides an indication that there are three main branches of Applied Translation, which are:

1. **Translation training**: This, as a branch of applied translation, encompasses teaching evolution methods, testing techniques and curriculum designs in translation studies. In the most recent two decades, there has been an increase in interest in the subject of translator training. Among the most essential aspects of textual interpretation is ensuring that quality is maintained throughout the translation process. The accumulation of the information and abilities essential to acquire proficiency in translation is what is referred to as translator training. Skills and expertise in the fields of

linguistics, translation, technology, interpersonal communication, and service providing are considered to be the primary areas of proficiency. Training for translators can take many different shapes. On the job training, feedback from supervisors, peers, evaluators, and customers, as well as the opportunity to make mistakes and learn from them, are all important ways to gain knowledge. As a result of the fact that the overwhelming preponderance of skilled translators around the globe undoubtedly do not have any instruction in translation other than their own experience, the importance of gaining experience should not be understated. This would be the very first degree of instruction that one would receive. At the next stage, there is a growing number of comprehensive induction classes, both in-house as well as on the private sector, that offer translators the tools they require to shift from one professional specialty to another. These courses can be found in a variety of settings. Courses like these might focus on recent developments in translation technology, terminology specialized to a certain field, project management, or different communicative skills, particularly as they relate to the various forms of translating.

2. **Translation Aid**: This has been discussed extensively here, mainly the machine translation. However, machine translation is no only the component of translation aided system. Areas such as translation software, online databases and use of internet are recognized areas. When it comes to translating text, businesses now have a legitimate alternative to employing a human translator, and that alternative is the use of machine translation software. Machine translation software, also referred to as MT software, is a utility that is built on artificial intelligence and provides automatic interpretations of text between various languages, for instance from English to Spanish or conversely. This type of software is also known as MT software. At the time it was invented, software for machine translation did not have the greatest translation precision; however, technological advancements over the half a century have ensured that such operating system can now do a job that is relatively accurate. As a consequence of this, the software that falls under this category is frequently incorporated into computer-assisted translation (CAT) tools, which are utilized by businesses that are engaged in the development of international initiatives. For instance, multinational businesses that want to customize their websites may use software that translates massive quantities of text at once, such as machine translation programs.

Nevertheless, MT software is put to use for a variety of translation purposes beyond just website localization. In addition to this, it is able to transcribe legal documents, such as contracts and other supporting materials, which are necessary to maintain profitable business relationships on an international scale. And the financial upside of investing in translation is clear: according to a survey conducted by "Common Sense Advisory" (CSA Investigation). This finding was based on a comparison of businesses that spent more on translation to those that didn't spend as much on translation.

3. **Translation Criticism**: This is another significant area in applied translation. The term "translation criticism" refers to the analytical process of analyzing and translating translated texts. It is a branch of academia that draws from literature studies and language studies. Student versions are graded, and evaluations of professional texts are analyzed. Newmark (1988) argues that there are two aspects of a translation to evaluate critically: referential and linguistic errors. Evidence, the physical world, and ideas, not words, are at the heart of a case of faulty reference. An integral component of translation studies, translation criticism bridges the gap between theoretical and practical considerations of the translation process. In order to be as unbiased, empirical, and fair as possible, it is important to have this type of assessment prevent vague and blind, as well as random criticism, and instead examine and evaluate the translation procedure and outcome factually, comprehensively, and systematically in light of certain theories.

Reviews of translations ought to think about everything that goes into making them. While it does incorporate some forms of critique, such as study and reading of the ST, it is distinct from those forms of criticism. Criticism of a translation should go beyond the simple detection of mistakes and into a more nuanced and nuanced evaluation of the translation's quality and accuracy.

There are different types of critique that can be applied to a translation, such as the practical, critical, and comparison. One could argue that functional critique is a form of emotional evaluation. Critical analysis takes a step back and examines the work critically. There will be a thorough comparison between the source text and every single word in the transcript. Translations, both good and bad, are discussed and critiqued. The term "contrast critique" is used to describe the process of evaluating the quality, accuracy, and consistency of translations by comparing multiple copies produced by various translators. This allows the translation to build on its successes while avoiding its failures, to extract its substance while leaving behind its fat, and to work in harmony with its source text. Practical and academic considerations alike should be taken into account when considering translation criticism's purpose. "The most fundamental function of translation critique is the managerial function, from which it draws the directing functions for users and for translators", says the author. Theoretical investigation is the second primary role of translation critique.

Works Cited

Almutawa, F., & Izwaini, S. (2015). Machine Translation in the Arab World: Saudi Arabia as a Case Study. http://www.trans-kom.eu/bd08nr02/trans-kom_08_02_04_Almutawa_Izwaini_MT.20151211.pdf.

Baker, M., and Saldanha, G (2000) Routledge Encyclopedia of Translation Studies, London: Routledge.

Chéragui, M. A. (2012) Theoretical overview of machine translation. Paper presented at the Proceedings ICWIT.

Dai, H., Xhafa, F., Janse, B.J., LIang, H. and Ye, J. (2022) "Comparative analysis of machine translation and human translation under the background of the Internet", International Conference on Cognitive-based Information Processing and Applications (CIPA 2021), *1*(84), pp.877–882.

Davis, P. (Oxford, 2008; online edn, Oxford Academic, 1 Jan. 2009). 'CHAPTER 3 Dryden and the Bounds of Liberty', Translation and the Poet's Life: The Ethics of Translating in English Culture, 1646-1726.

Delavenay, É. (1960) An Introduction to Machine Translation. London: Thames and Hudson.

Denkowski, M. (2015) Machine Translation for Human Translators. (PhD Doctoral Dissertation), Carnegie Mellon University.

Dai, H., Xhafa, F., Janse, B.J., LIang, H. and Ye, J. (2022), "Comparative analysis of machine translation and human translation under the background of the Internet", International Conference on Cognitive-based Information Processing and Applications (CIPA 2021), Vol. 1 No. 84, pp. 877-882.

Erjavec, T. Z. (2003) Compilation and exploitation of parallel corpora. CIT, Journal of Computing and Information Technology, *11*(2) pp.93–102.

Gerber, L. (2012), "Machine Translation: ingredients for productive and stable MT deployments – Part 2", available at: www.translationdirectory.com.

Gnecchi, M., Maylath, B., Scarpa, F., Mousten, B., and Vandepitte, S. (2011) "Field Convergence: Merging Roles of Technical Writers and Technical Translators", IEEE-Transactions on Professional Communication, *54*. pp.168-184.

Holmes, J. S. (2000) "The name and nature of translation studies", in The Translation Studies Reader, L. Venuti (ed.) London: Routledge. pp. 180–92.

Holmes, J. (2002). Translation Studies. London: Blackwell Publishers.

Holmström, J.E. (1951) Report on interlingual scientific and technical dictionaries. Paris: UNESCO.

Homiedan, A. H. (1998) "Machine translation", Journal of King Saud University, Language & Translation, *10*. pp. 1–21.

Hutchins, J. (2001) "Machine translation and human translation: in competition or in complementation?", International Journal of Translation, *13*(1-2) pp. 5–20.

Hutchins, W. J. (1995) "Machine translation: A brief history", in Concise history of the language sciences: from the Sumerians to the cognitivists, E. F. K. Koerner and R. E. Asher (eds.) Oxford: Pergamon Press. pp. 431–445.

Khalilizadeh, M. (2016) A comparative study on translation of homonyms done by translation machines (A Case study of Google Translate and I'm translator websites). Paper presented at the National Conference on Translation and interdisciplinary Studies, Birjand University, Birjand, Iran.

Kong, L. (2022). Artificial Intelligence-Based Translation Technology in Translation Teaching. Computational Intelligence and Neuroscience, 2022, 1–9. https://doi.org/10.1155/2022/6016752

Maghsoudi, M. and Mirzaeian, V. (2020), "Machine versus human translation outputs: which one results in better reading comprehension among EFL learners?", The JALT CALL Journal, Vol. 16 No. 2, pp. 69-84, doi: 10.29140/jaltcall.v16n2.342.

McEnery, T., and Wilson, A. (1993) Corpora and Translation: Uses and Future Prospects. UCREL.

McEnery, T. and Hardie, A. (2012) Corpus Linguistics: Method, Theory, and Practice, Cambridge Univ. Press, Cambridge, 1st edition, doi: 10.1017/CBO9780511981395.

McGillivray, B. and Kilgarriff, A. (2013) "Tools for historical corpus research, and a corpus of Latin", in New Methods in Historical Corpus Linguistics, P. Bennett, M. Durrell, S. Scheible, and R.J. Whitt (eds.) Tübingen: Narr.

Mendel, Y. (2016) "German orientalism, Arabic grammar and the Jewish education system: the origins and effect of Martin Plessner's 'theory of Arabic grammar'", Naharaim, *10*(1) pp. 57–77, doi: 10.1515/naha-2016-0004.

Munkova, D., Munk, M., Welnitzova, K., and Jakabovicova, J. (2021) "Product and process analysis of machine translation into the inflectional language", SAGE Open, *11*(4) doi: 10.1177/21582440211054501.

Munday, J. (2008) Introducing Translation Studies: Theories and Applications, USA and Canada: Routledge, 2nd edition.

Li, H., Graesser, A. C. and Cai, Z. (2014) "Comparison of Google translation with human translation", Paper presented at Twenty-Seventh International Florida Artificial Intelligence Research Society Conference, USA.

Papineni, K., Roukos, S., Ward, T., & Zhu, W.-J. (2002). BLEU: a Method for Automatic Evaluation of Machine Translation. https://aclanthology.org/P02-1040.pdf

Şahin, M. and Gürses, S. (2021), "English-Turkish literary translation through human-machine interaction", Revista Tradumàtica, Vol. 19, pp. 306-310, doi: 10.5565/rev/tradumatica.284.

Shuttleworth, M., & Cowie, M. (2014) Dictionary of Translation Studies, New York: Routledge.

Somers, H. (2003) Computers and translation: a translator's guide, Amsterdam and Philadelphia: John Benjamins Publishing Company.

Toury, G. (1995) Descriptive translation studies – and beyond, Amsterdam and Philadelphia: John Benjamins Publishing Co, revised edition.

Venuti, L. (ed.) (2004). The Translation Studies Reader. USA and Canada: Routledge.

Urlaub, P., & Dessein, E. (2022). Machine translation and foreign language education. Frontiers in Artificial Intelligence, 5. https://doi.org/10.3389/frai.2022.936111

Wilks, Y. (2009) Machine Translation: Its Scope and Limits: Springer.

Vasheghani Farahani, M. (2020) "Adequacy in machine vs human translation: a comparative study of English and Persian languages", Applied Linguistics Research Journal, *4*(5) pp. 84–104, doi: 10.14744/alrj.2020.98700.

Vieira, L.N. and Alonso, E. (2020) "Translating perceptions and managing expectations: an analysis of management and production perspectives on machine translation", Perspectives, *28*(2) pp. 163–184, doi: 10.1080/0907676X.2019.1646776.

Waddington, C. (2001) "Different methods of evaluating student translations: the question of validity, Meta", Translators' Journal, *46*(2) pp. 311–325.

Way, A. (2018), "Quality expectations of machine translation", in Translation Quality Assessment, J. Moorkens, S. Castilho, F. Gaspari, and S. Doherty (eds.) Cham: Springer. pp. 159–178, doi: 10.48550/arXiv.1803.08409.

CONCLUSIONS

Translation remains a significant component of our everyday communication. The production of a textbook that contains critical issues in translation attends to the generality of communication between people that speak different languages. This textbook expounded on a variety of topics that bordered on what makes translation an applied discipline, what differentiates translation theory and theories of translation, and what differentiates different branches of applied translation, including the fundamental topics in machine translation and the generality of technology in translation. As the focus of contemporary discussion on translation was on translation studies and applied translation, this textbook expounded on these topics. The textbook makes clear two particularly prominent aspects that have played a role in elevating translation studies to a more prominent academic field in recent years. At both the undergraduate and graduate levels, there has been a meteoric rise in the number of specialized translation and translating classes that are being made available to students. The primary focus of these programs is the education of future specialists in translation, who are capable of working in professional settings, which collectively attract thousands of students each year. In addition, they serve as extremely valuable qualifications for entry-level translators and translators to begin their careers.

Significantly, the authors of the textbook have made great statements on arrays of issues in translation but dwelt more on the topic of the application of technology in translation. The application of technology in translation is one area of applied translation that has developed over the years and continues to be relevant in contemporary discourses in translation. This topic, which can be discussed under the umbrella of machine translation, is an example of an area that has remained relevant. According to Holmes (2002), the acceptance of machine translation within the more general field of applied translation is predicated on the projection of the concept of "use", which refers to the manner in which a computer or other piece of technology is utilized to either facilitate the translation of texts or translate texts themselves. It is therefore important to advance the conversation about machine translation, concentrating primarily on how machine translation has supported human translators in delivering appropriate and environmentally motivated counterparts to the texts that were originally translated. In spite of the fact that new technologies do not present an original theoretical framework, the book sheds light on how they have had a significant influence on translation and how they are presently influencing both its research and its theoretical development. It addressed how there has been an increase in the demand for translation services as a result of the increasing significance of interregional collaboration and the need to share information. This rise in demand has been brought about as a result of the need to share information. There is a significant portion of the material that needs to be translated. The vast majority of this endeavor is dull and repetitive, requiring accuracy and steadiness in performance; however, certain facets of it are challenging and difficult. As the need for translation continues to rise, it is becoming increasingly difficult for qualified translators to keep up with the demand. In this particular setting, machine translation has proven to be of significant assistance.

The concerns that technological breakthroughs in translation may one day eliminate the need for human translators were also investigated in this research. The primary objective of this study was to provide an explanation of the question of whether or not machine translation could successfully replace human translators or work in conjunction with them. This question has received much attention in recent conversations about new developments and shifts in technology's role in translation. Although MT has significantly impacted the translation industry, the researchers concluded that human translation efforts would not be superseded by machine translators and will continue to be present in the years to come. This was the conclusion reached by the study. The authors went to the further conclusion that translators' connections with Machine Translator and pessimistic perceptions against it may transform in a favorable manner as MT continues to advance and translation practice continues to develop. This was due to the fact that MT is far from being an essential component of any literary translation exercise.

In conclusion, translating is a continuous struggle between remaining truthful to the source text and remaining truthful to the target message. This requires not just to respecting the culture of the target language but also the society and the norms of the language being translated into. Because of this, translating a document is a challenging undertaking that does not have right or wrong solutions, but rather a variety of viewpoints and techniques to take. The introduction of the culture is one of the more challenging aspects of translation because it is precisely in these kinds of circumstances that adaptation is required and where the translator is put in the position of attempting to captivate every member of the target audience, which is not an easy objective to accomplish.

There is an extensive culture that translators need to consider to carry out linguistic transfer. Training in linguistics, literature, history, and culture are all required for this. In addition, it is essential to keep in mind that the purpose of translation is to convey the significance of an article in its original language into another language while avoiding the influence of societal biases, which could cause us to alter the meaning of the text we are translating. In conclusion, the role of the translator is to facilitate communication, despite the fact that the materials we are working with come from two distinct linguistic and cultural systems. This must be done while bearing in mind that flawless lexical cohesion somehow doesn't occur in language, and in light of this, it stands to reason that translators have the final say, as they are the only people responsible for the creative work involved in translation.

This textbook covered a wide variety of subjects, including those that bordered on the nature of the topic of translation, the historical periods in translation, the theories of translation, the strategies in translation that have been developed from different approaches, a discussion of various concepts that are prominent in translation, and further exploration of various trends in applied translation. The content of the book is organized in such a way that both students and specialists in translation will have access to a wide variety of information that is both important and relevant regarding historical and current problems in translation.